Foreword

The former National Heritage Council, under the chairmanship of Lord Killanin, commissioned An Taisce in 1993 to prepare an evaluation of environmental designations in Ireland. The study led to the publication, by An Taisce, in 1994, of a booklet entitled Environmental Designations in Ireland, which outlined the basis for 20 different environmental designations in Ireland. The publication of the booklet was supported by the award, to An Taisce, of an Environmental Awareness Award by the Department of the Environment.

On receipt of the final detailed report from An Taisce by the Heritage Council (established on a statutory basis by Minister Michael D. Higgins, TD., on July 10th, 1995), the Council decided that it should publish the valuable information contained in the report. In doing so, the Heritage Council also included a number of specific and general recommendations designed to improve both the efficiency of the environmental designation process in Ireland and the enforcement of environmental designations.

The Heritage Council recognises the difficulties encountered by local authority personnel, non-governmental organisations, and the general public in keeping abreast of the plethora of environmental designations arising from recent European Union and national legislation. In publishing this report, the Heritage Council wishes to review existing designations and provide readily accessible information on their content.

In a time of increased interest in, and awareness of environmental issues, it is hoped that this report will make a positive contribution to the on-going development of realistic environmental strategies at local, regional and national levels.

Freda Rountree
Chairperson, July 1996

Foreword to the Second Edition

This publication is being reprinted because of demand sometimes from unexpected quarters, which underlines the central role that natural heritage is beginning to play in the economic life of this country. The designation of Special Areas of Conservation highlights that new awareness of environment. By and large, landowners, as primary custodians of heritage, are accepting that responsibility, and are developing enthusiasm for schemes like the Rural Environmental Protection Scheme. This enthusiasm is greater than the economic rewards gained by them from that scheme. Let us hope that the great love of land which is built in the Irish people will transfer to the protection of their environment.

Freda Rountree
Chairperson, July 1997

Réamhrá

D'údaraigh an Chomhairle Oidhreachta a bhí ann faoi Chathaoirleacht an Tiarna Cill Ainnín don Taisce i 1993 luacháil ar ainmniúcháin chomhshaoil in Éirinn a ullmhú. As an staidéar sin tháinig leabhrán a d'fhoilsigh an Taisce i 1994 dar teideal Environmental Designations in Ireland, a leag amach bunús do 20 ainmniúchán comhshaoil in Éirinn. Chuidigh gradam, an Gradam Feasachta Comhshaoil ón Roinn Comhshaoil a fuair an Taisce le foilsiú an leabhráin.

Nuair a fuair an Chomhairle Oidhreachta (ar chuir an tAire Micheál D. Ó hUiginn bunús reachtúil léi an 10ú Iúil 1995) an miontuarascáil chríochnaitheach ón Taisce shocraigh an Chomhairle gur cheart di an t-eolas luachmhar a bhí sa tuarascáil a fhoilsiú. Agus í a dhéanamh sin chuir an Chomhairle roinnt moltaí sonracha agus ginearálta a bhí leagtha amach chun feabhas a chur ar éifeachtacht an phróisis ainmniúchán comhshaoil in Éirinn agus fheidhmiú ainmniúchán comhshaoil san áireamh.

Aithníonn an Chomhairle Oidhreachta na deacrachtaí a bhíonn ag daoine sna údaráis áitiúla, ag eagraíochtaí nach eagraíochtaí rialtais iad, agus ag an bpobal go ginearálta coinneáil suas leis an lear mór ainmniúchán comhshaoil a tháinig as reachtaíocht ón Aontas Eorpach agus ó reachtaíocht náisiúnta le gairid. Agus iad ag foilsiú na tuarasála seo tá an Chomhairle ag iarraidh na hainmniúcháin atá ann a athbhreithniú agus eolas atá inrochtana go héasca a chur ar fáil ar an méid atá iontu.

Agus tuiscint níos mó ar cheisteanna comhshaoil agus spéis níos mó a chur iontu tá súil go gcuideoidh an tuarascáil seo ar bhealach dearfach le forbairt leanúnach ar straitéisí comhshaoil réalacha ag na leibhéil náisiúnacha, réigiúnacha agus áitiúla.

Freda Rountree
Cathaoirleach, Iúil 1996

Réamhrá don Dara hEagrán

Tá athchló á dhéanamh ar an bhfoilseachán seo de bharr éileamh a bheith air go minic ó áiteanna agus ó dhaoine nach mbeadh súil leis rud a léiríonn an ról láithreach atá anois ag an oidhreacht nádúrtha i saol eacnamaíoch na tíre. Léiríonn ainmniú na Limistéar Caomhnaithe Speisialta an tuiscint nua sin faoin gcomhshaol. Tríd is tríd tá lucht talún arb iad coiméadaithe na hoidhreachta go príomha iad ag glacadh leis an bhfreagracht sin agus tá siad ag cur spéise i scéimeanna mar an Scéim Chosanta Comhshaoil Tuaithe. Is mó í an spéis sin ná an luach saothair eacnamaíoch a fhaigheann siad ón scéim sin. Bíodh dóchas againn go léireofar an ghean ar an talamh is dual do mhuintir na hÉireann i gcosaint an chomhshaoil.

Freda Rountree
Cathaoirleach, Iúil 1997

Contents

Preface to Second Edition

Since the publication of the first edition, in July 1996, there have been a number of policy developments which the Heritage Council considers sufficiently important to be included in a second edition. These are:

—   The Special Area of Conservation (SAC), referred to in the first edition as a *proposed* designation, has been given legal status since February 1997, in compliance with the EU Habitats Directive. Approximately 400 SACs are expected to be designated. Formal designation is expected to begin in the latter half of 1997 (see pages 27-28). Additional recommendations made by the Heritage Council on SACs are included on pages 100-102.

—   31 additional Special Protection Areas (SPAs) have been designated in compliance with the EU Birds Directive (see Table 2.3, page 22, and Figure 2.2, page 25).

—   26 additional Ramsar Sites have been designated, all of which overlap with SPAs (see pages 45-46).

—   Several National Parks (Wicklow Mountains and Glenveagh) have continued to expand, and the process of creating a sixth park in Mayo is underway, following the publication of a feasibility study. The National Parks and Wildlife Service continues to acquire land in the Owenduff/Nephin area as a nucleus for the proposed park (see pages 35 -41).

—   The Environmentally Sensitive Area (ESA) designation, applied solely to two small pilot areas, has been phased out and replaced by the Rural Environment Protection Scheme (REPS) (see pages 84-88).

—   Further changes have been made to the Rural Environment Protection Scheme (REPS) *within designated areas* to combat overgrazing and conserve wildlife (see pages 86-87).

—   In January 1997, the Department of Environment has proposed to allow local authorities to designate areas sensitive to forestry development. No further details are available at the time of writing.

—   The Minister for the Environment has proposed a Special Amenity Area Order (SAAO) for part of the Howth peninsula in Co. Dublin (see pages 63-64).

—   Skellig Michael was designated as Ireland's second UNESCO World Heritage Site in December 1996.

At the time of writing, the Wildlife Act, 1976 has still not been amended and, as such, the Natural Heritage Area (NHA) remains a *proposed* designation. This means that some hundreds of such sites remain effectively unprotected apart from those which have other protective designations (see pages 15-20).

The Government's National Sustainable Development Plan, published in April, 1997, contains a commitment to give a statutory basis to NHAs, but no target date has been set. The Plan also contains a commitment to designate and protect SACs, and promises to publish the National Parks and Heritage Bill in 1997, to give statutory recognition to, inter alia, National Parks.

D. Hickie, Author
July, 1997

Section 1
Introduction

8

Introduction

What are environmental designations? A designation marks out an area or feature of special interest or value which stands out from the remainder. 'Environmental' in the context of this report includes nature, the landscape and amenities. Over the last 20 years, many designations have been made for different objectives, but these have rarely been evaluated.

Who is responsible? Responsibility for all environmental designations made in Ireland lies with local authorities and/or Government departments. The European Union oversees the implementation of EU designations by Member States. International bodies oversee a number of designations made as a result of inter-governmental agreements, such as the United Nations, the Council of Europe and the Ramsar Secretariat.

How does one encounter environmental designations? Most designations are encountered through involvement in planning

Brent Geese over Sandymount Strand, designated as a Special Protection Area for Birds.

and development matters. For example, a developer searching for a factory site may decide to locate outside a designated amenity area so as to facilitate planning permission; a person planning to build a house in a designated scenic area may find restrictions on the design and siting of his building; or a landowner's eligibility for development grants may be affected.

Glen of the Downs Nature Reserve.

OVERVIEW OF ENVIRONMENTAL DESIGNATIONS

The objectives and scope of the designations examined in this report are given below.

Table 1.1 Objectives and scope of designations

1.	Natural Heritage Area (NHA) (proposed)	Conservation of plants, animals and wildlife habitats of Irish importance. All other nature designations are sub-sets of NHAs.
2.	Special Protection Area (SPA)	Conservation of rare and threatened bird species and their habitats in the European Union.
3.	Special Area of Conservation (SAC)	Conservation of plants, animals and wildlife habitats of European Union importance.
4.	Statutory Nature Reserve	Strict conservation of plants, animals and wildlife habitats to the exclusion of all other activities.
5.	National Park	Nature conservation and public use and appreciation.
6.	Refuge for Fauna	Conservation of the habitat of a particular animal species.
7.	Wildfowl Sanctuary	Hunting of wild birds prohibited.
8.	Ramsar Site	Conservation of wetlands of international importance listed in the Ramsar Convention.
9.	Biogenetic Reserve	Conservation of biodiversity in sites recognised by the Council of Europe.
10.	UNESCO Biosphere Reserve	Nature conservation and sustainable development in sites recognised by UNESCO.
11.	Salmonid Water	Maintenance and improvement of water quality for salmon and trout.
12	Sensitive Area for Urban Wastewater	Improvement of water quality in areas suffering from pollution by installation or upgrading of sewage treatment.
13.	Sensitive Area for Fisheries and Forestry	Protection of sensitive rivers and lakes from forestry operations
14.	Area of Special Control in County Development Plan	Maintenance of scenic qualities and amenity value on a county basis.
15.	Special Amenity Area Order (SAAO)	Strict controls over development in areas of high scenic and amenity value.
16.	Tree Preservation Order (TPO)	Protection of trees and woods of special amenity value.
17.	World Heritage Site	Conservation of sites or features of global environmental and/or heritage value recognised by UNESCO.
18.	Designated Area under the Rural Environment Protection Scheme (REPS)	Promotion of environmentally sensitive farming by means of grants to farmers.

SCOPE OF DESIGNATIONS

The scope of each designation is listed below.

BACKGROUND TO NATURE AND LANDSCAPE CONSERVATION POLICY IN IRELAND

Ireland has been occupied by man for at least 9,000 years, and its landscapes and biotopes have been shaped by agriculture for at least 4,000 years. The island has been extensively deforested and is unusual in Europe (along with Scotland and Iceland) in having so much open, treeless landscape. Only tiny fragments of native forest, which once covered most of the island, survive and even these are not considered to be primeval. Ireland's biodiversity is naturally low, being an island outside the natural range of many continental European species, but there are unusual assemblages of species, such as in the Burren, and the island is one of the last outposts of peatlands in western Europe. Ireland is also important for its seabird colonies and migratory waterfowl.

Ireland is a 'late starter' in developing its conservation policies. It has the smallest area devoted to nature protection of any European

Table 1.2 Scope of Designations

DESIGNATION	NUMBER	COVERAGE [PROPOSED]
Natural Heritage Area (proposed)	1,251	(approx. 700,000 ha.)
Special Area of Conservation	400	(approx. 551,000 ha.)
Special Protection Area	106	205,300 ha.
Statutory Nature Reserve	78	18,095 ha. (1994 figures)
National Park	5	47,287 ha.
Refuge for Fauna	7	figures not available
Wildfowl Sanctuary	68	figures not available
Ramsar Site	47	70,550 ha.
Biogenetic Reserve	14	6,587 ha.
UNESCO Biosphere Reserve	2	11,500 ha.
Salmonid Water	22	n/a
Sensitive Area for Urban Wastewater	10	n/a
Sensitive Area for Fisheries and Forestry	n/a	approx. 5%
Area of Special Control in County Development Plan	n/a	figures not available
Special Amenity Area Order	2	under 2,000 ha.
Tree Preservation Order	178	n/a
World Heritage Site	2	803 ha.
Designated Area under the Rural Environment Protection Scheme	n/a	Degraded areas: west Mayo and Galway, parts of Donegal, Sligo and Kerry. All NHAs, SACs and Salmonid Waters.

country, and landscape protection policy is also poorly developed. The reasons for this are partly cultural. Private property rights are strongly defended in the Irish constitution. Ireland still has a strong rural vote, a folk memory of landlessness and colonisation, a large number of small rural owner-occupiers, and less experience of obvious environmental degradation until recently. Public support for conservation is higher in countries with large urban populations and experience of extensive environmental degradation. *The impetus to put in place a range of environmental policies has come mainly from the European Union and not from Irish administrations.* Thus, Ireland is reluctantly adopting the environmental policies of its Northern European neighbours as a quid pro quo for the economic benefits of membership of the European Union. In recent years, however, the Irish tourism and food sectors have recognised the value of environmental quality in promoting their products, which may give some political impetus to protect the landscape, water quality and wildlife.

TERMS OF REFERENCE

This report is based on a study commissioned by the National Heritage Council in 1993 to evaluate Irish environmental designations independently of government but with the cooperation of official bodies. No such evaluation has been made to date by the official bodies responsible. The purpose of the study was to examine the aims and objectives of each designation, identify interactions and overlaps between designations, and evaluate the effectiveness and potential of each designation. The brief also required an evaluation of environmental designations in the context of overall environmental policy and the presentation of recommendations for more effective and efficient application of designations where necessary.

STRUCTURE OF THE REPORT

The report is divided into seven main sections:

Section 1. Introduction
Section 2. Nature designations
Section 3. Amenity designations
Section 4. Water designations
Section 5. Other designations
Section 6. Analysis
Section 7. General conclusions and
            recommendations

Conclusions and recommendations are made for each designation and at the end of each section. General conclusions and recommendations are made in Sections 6 and 7. This report summarises the main study presented to the newly formed statutory Heritage Council in November 1995, but has been updated to June 1997.

Sand dunes, proposed for designation as an NHA, Donegal.

David Hickie

Section 2
Nature designations

Figure 2.1
Proposed Natural Heritage
Areas (NHAs).
Source: NPWS.
(Reproduced by kind
permission of the Minister
for Arts, Culture and the
Gaeltacht.)

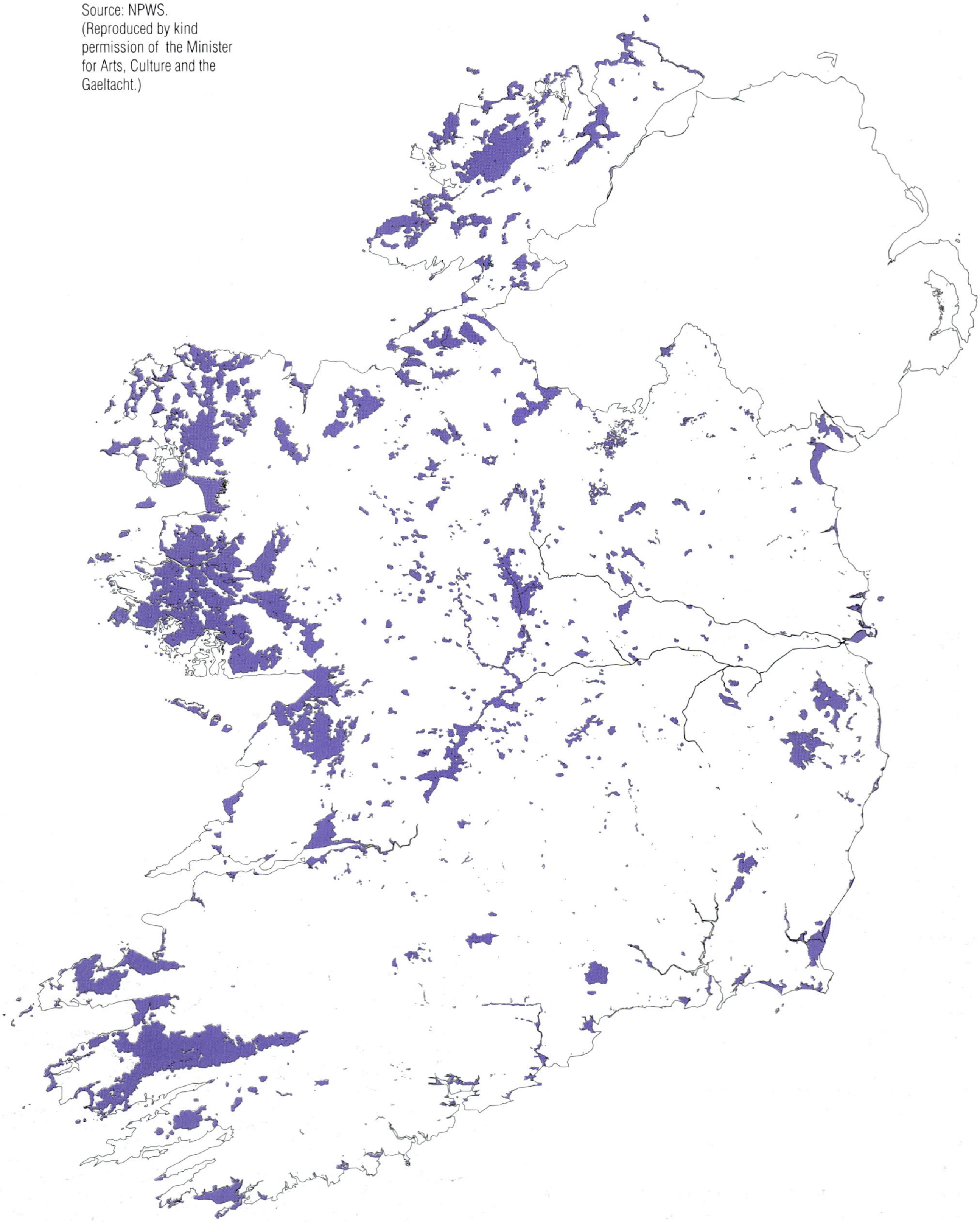

2.1

Natural Heritage Area (NHA)
(proposed)

OBJECTIVE Protection of natural habitats in Ireland.
LEGAL BACKING None. Wildlife Act (Amendment) Bill is forthcoming.
COVERAGE Approx. 700,000 ha. of land and water; 1,251 sites.
RESPONSIBLE AUTHORITY National Parks and Wildlife Service, Dept. of Arts, Culture and the Gaeltacht.
POWERS UNDER DESIGNATION Until the Wildlife Act 1976 is amended, no legal power to prevent damaging activities, except developments covered by the Planning Acts.

BACKGROUND

The Natural Heritage Area (NHA) designation is the base of the system for protection of Irish natural habitats. All other nature designations overlap with NHAs. The NHA is a proposed designation and has no legal basis until the Wildlife Amendment Bill is passed.

Evolution of the NHA designation Places where plants and animals exist in a relatively natural state are given a higher value by ecologists than habitats highly modified by human activity. NHAs include the best of Ireland's remaining natural habitats (see Figure 2.1). The NHA designation evolved from the Area of Scientific Interest (ASI) designation. The purpose of ASIs was to identify — not designate — natural areas as a guide for planning authorities. ASIs were surveyed and mapped by An Foras Forbartha (AFF) on a county basis in the 1970s. In 1981, AFF published a national review of ASIs, one of the aims of which was "to act as a baseline against which future changes in the quality or importance of sites can be measured" (AFF, 1981). In 1987, responsibility was transferred to the Office of Public Works (OPW), which continued to list new ASIs and re-define existing sites. By 1989, almost 1,500 ASIs were mapped and listed, and circulated to all official and voluntary bodies. Sites were termed ASIs until 1992 and thereafter termed NHAs, a title which was felt to be more descriptive.

The High Court in 1992 found that a particular ASI (Roundstone Bog, Co. Galway) was in fact a designation, and not merely an identification, since the landowners involved were refused forestry grants and refused planning permission because of the site's status as an ASI. This was found to be unconstitutional and was quashed because it was made without due notice to the owners, who had no opportunity to object. This landmark decision precipitated a major re-survey of 80% of listed ASIs by the OPW from 1992 to 1994. The National Parks and Wildlife Service (NPWS), currently the conservation authority, proposed these for designation as Natural Heritage Areas in 1995/6 and proposed to allow landowners to be notified and to have the opportunity to object.

EVALUATION

Monitoring the 'health' of sites Since the early 1970s, there has been little official monitoring of the ecological condition of listed sites. A survey of the 80 ASIs in Co. Donegal in 1983 showed that 25% were damaged or threatened (Cabot, 1985). A more recent assessment (1983 to 1991) found 37% of surveyed sites damaged and a further 16% under immediate threat (Nairn, 1992) (see Table 2.1).

Blanket bog degraded by overgrazing, Erriff Valley, Co. Mayo.

David Hickie

Natural Heritage Areas

Ian Lawler

Traditionally managed grassland, Inisheer, Co. Galway.

Rahasane turlough, Co. Galway. Many turloughs have been drained, and some remain under threat. Turloughs are important for wintering waterfowl.

Con O'Rourke

Sand dunes at Machaire Uí Robhartaigh, Co. Donegal. Sand dune systems are under threat from recreational pressure, golf courses and agricultural intensification.

David Hickie

Intact blanket bog, Fiddandarrry, Co. Sligo. Government policy is to refuse grant-aid for afforestation of NHAs, especially peatlands. The main current threats to blanket bogs are turf extraction and overgrazing.

David Hickie

16

Table 2.1   Damage or threat to Areas of Scientific Interest in four counties in Ireland 1983-1991 (after Nairn, 1992)

COUNTY	NO. OF ASIS LISTED (1989)	NO. OF ASIS SURVEYED (1983-91)	NO. OF ASIS DAMAGED[1]	NO. OF ASIS UNDER THREAT[2]
Donegal	119	83	30 (36%)	9 (11%)
Sligo	42	41	15 (36%)	7 (17%)
Wexford	38	33	13 (39%)	5 (15%)
Wicklow	60	37	14 (38%)	11 (18%)
TOTAL	259	194	72 (37%)	32 (16%)

1. Damage is defined as any significant loss of scientific interest.
2. Threat is defined as any immediate threat to scientific interest.

Only two of the causes of damage required planning permission at that time (see Table 2.2). The remaining causes were exempt and it was clear that the ASI designation had little or no effect in preventing damage. Indeed, landowners were mostly not aware that their land was of ecological interest.

Agricultural activities caused the most damage, along with recreation and afforestation. In Great Britain up to 1991, agriculture, recreation and miscellaneous other activities were the main causes of damage to the equivalent designation: Sites of Special Scientific Interest.

GOVERNMENT POLICY FOR PROTECTION OF NHAs/ASIs

The NHA system currently lacks any legislative backing, unlike similar site protection systems abroad. Less than 10% by area of listed NHAs (mainly woods, bogs and intertidal areas) are legally protected *only* because they are in Nature Reserves or National Parks.

Grant aid policy

• From 1981, EU drainage and reclamation grants in ASIs were refused funding by the Dept. of Agriculture if the Forest and Wildlife Service considered them to be

Table 2.2   Principal recorded causes of damage to Areas of Scientific Interest in four sample counties in Ireland, 1983-1991 (after Nairn, 1992)

ACTIVITY	NUMBER OF ASIS AFFECTED*				
	DONEGAL	SLIGO	WEXFORD	WICKLOW	TOTAL
Recreational pressure	1	5	3	3	12
Afforestation	4	0	1	3	8
Water pollution	2	1	5	0	8
Overgrazing	4	4	0	0	8
Drainage	4	0	1	2	7
Sports/golf courses	4	2	0	1	7
Quarrying/mining	3	1	0	3	7
Tree felling	5	1	0	1	7
Housing development	1	3	0	1	5
Coastal erosion	1	1	2	1	5
Peat cutting	2	1	0	1	4
Fencing	3	0	0	0	3
Road building	2	0	0	0	2

* Some ASIs are subject to more than one damaging activity

damaging. This was to comply with a clause in the EU Programme for Western Development (75/628/EEC) that EU funds should not damage the environment. Only a minority of grants were refused.

- From 1990 onwards, the Forest Service has generally refused EU grants for afforestation in ASIs/NHAs in order to comply with EU regulations governing the use of EU funds for forestry.

- In 1994, the Rural Environment Protection Scheme (REPS) was launched (see Section 5.1) to pay farmers for protecting wildlife and the landscape. Farmers who own NHAs are eligible for an extra 20% on the basic annual payment.

- In other areas where EU funds were involved, official policy has not been as unambiguous. From the early 1970s to the late 1980s, Office of Public Works arterial drainage schemes and Forest and Wildlife Service afforestation projects damaged a number of listed sites, mainly peatlands, turloughs and other wetlands. A number of EU Structural-funded golf courses and road schemes have damaged listed sites during the 1990s.

Local authority policy From the late 1980s, most local authority Development Plans included a list of ASIs. Analysis of sample planning decisions affecting ASIs up to 1995 indicated that the listed sites were not generally respected as 'no go areas' for damaging developments. Indeed, the 1995 Cork County Development Plan states that

"... listing in the development plan is not always sufficient by itself to protect areas from development pressures, and land of high scenic amenity or ecological value but low agricultural value is particularly under threat".

"The need for a means of acquiring and managing sensitive or ecologically important areas is becoming increasingly pressing".

"Over the years, there has been no diminution in the threats to these amenities and reliance solely on controls has not been as effective as circumstances would merit. Active involvement by the State, the

Council and other interested parties will be necessary to ensure an adequate level of protection".

"The Council considers that legislative changes are required to address this matter."

National Parks and Wildlife Service policy
The Wildlife Act, 1976 was written before the need for a site safeguard system was officially recognised. Thus, it was assumed that the authorities had no powers to protect sites which were not State-owned Nature Reserves. However, the Wildlife Act does allow the Minister to make management agreements. Only two such agreements are currently in place. Thus, since 1976, successive Irish Governments were empowered to protect any site of ecological interest using management agreements, but in practice chose not to do so except through the small Nature Reserve network.

The NPWS is consulted by other Government departments on planning and grant applications which impinge on NHAs. Until the early 1990s, it was not the custom of the NPWS to make formal appeals against planning decisions. This has now changed. The NPWS recommends against most afforestation grants in NHAs. Regional staff assess many local developments, but without guidelines. A number of habitats have been damaged following assessment by the National Parks and Wildlife Service.

FORTHCOMING LEGISLATION
The Wildlife Act (Amendment) Bill is expected to require formal designation of NHAs and notification of owners, which will include the listing of damaging operations. If an owner wishes to carry out any such operations, he will be legally required to inform the NPWS. He may be legally prevented from undertaking such an operation for a limited period, during which the NPWS can negotiate a management agreement or site purchase. Objections will be entertained, but only on a scientific basis. If, at the end of the statutory period, the owner wishes to proceed with a damaging development, he may not be legally prevented

DESIGNATION OF NATURAL AREAS IN NORTHERN IRELAND

- Areas of Special Scientific Interest (ASSI) are administered in Northern Ireland by the Department of the Environment (NI), Countryside and Wildlife Branch.

- ASSIs have legislative backing in the Nature Conservation and Amenity Lands (Northern Ireland) Order 1985.

- 87 ASSIs were designated by February 1996, covering 75,185 ha. or under 0.6% of the territory. This is considered to be about two-thirds of the total area likely to be designated. There were 22 management agreements covering ASSIs in place by 1994.

- A system of monitoring will be put in place as the designation programme proceeds to ensure that the scientific interest of SSSIs is maintained. No official evaluation of ASSIs has been undertaken to date.

- Site management plans have been prepared for those ASSIs which will also be designated as SACs and SPAs (see Sections 2.2 and 2.3). Plans for the remaining ASSIs are expected by March 1997.

- The opinion of the Royal Society for the Protection of Birds, which has published an assessment of the performance of the ASSI designation in 1996, is that, although some damaging activities occur, destruction of sites is rare, and the designation works reasonably well.

Source: *Environment Service Corporate Plan* 1994-97; Mellon and Davidson, 1996

from so doing. The notification process is expected to take roughly several years. Sites of geological and geomorphological interest are expected to be covered.

RESOURCES ALLOCATED TO NHA PROGRAMME

In 1990 there were 91 staff working directly in the National Parks and Wildlife Service: Administration 20; Research 12; Wildlife Management 59. Five contract ecologists were employed to co-ordinate the 1992-94 national ASI/NHA survey. No additional staff are expected to be employed to deal with the extra workload involved in the notification process. Since objections will only be entertained on scientific grounds, it is not clear who will process these unless the scientific staff are asked to take on this workload in addition to their existing functions. The role of the NPWS in the Rural Environment Protection Scheme is referred to in Section 5.1.

COMPARISONS WITH SITE SAFEGUARD NETWORK IN UK

Designation and notification in the UK The Wildlife and Countryside Act 1981 required a major re-notification process for Sites of Special Scientific Interest (SSSIs) in Britain — the equivalent of NHAs. Ten years after the passing of the 1981 Act, the re-notification of SSSIs in England was 98% complete (English Nature 1992). A major difference between the proposed notification procedure in Ireland and the UK system is that landowners are notified of the intention to designate a site, with an opportunity for objections, after which time the site designation is either confirmed or withdrawn. The proposed procedure for Ireland is to publish a notice that a site has been designated, to notify the owner/occupiers by post, and to leave the onus on the owner/occupiers to object if they wish. The system operating in Northern Ireland is shown in the box above.

Natural sites in Ireland continue to suffer damage: drainage of raised bog in Co. Longford.

David Hickie

Site protection and management agreements in UK The main reason for the reluctance of the Irish Government to use management agreements to protect NHAs is the potential cost of annual payments to landowners. In Northern Ireland, management agreements have been used for 22 sites. The cumulative cost of maintaining management agreements in SSSIs in Scotland had reached almost £4.5 million (£37 per hectare) by 1993/94.

In England, there are now some 3,707 SSSIs. Owners of SSSIs are legally required to advise the conservation authority (English Nature) if they propose to undertake potentially damaging activities. If these are refused, English Nature can offer compensation by means of a management agreement. By 1993 there were over 1,700 management agreements in England, costing over £7 million per year. Management agreements covered only 7% of SSSI land area in England but, of the remaining area, a further 7% is already in National Nature Reserves, 14% is looked after by voluntary bodies and over 20% is owned by government bodies (Bourn, 1994).

SITE PROTECTION IN DENMARK

Denmark's system of protected areas has some similarities with the proposed Irish system. *All* semi-natural habitats, including sand dunes, grasslands, wetlands and woodlands have some protection under the Danish Nature Protection Act, 1992: landowners are permitted to continue with their existing land use, but not to intensify, and there is no compensation for any losses that may be incurred. Compensation is given when landowners are asked by the conservation authorities to change their land use (e.g. convert from arable to grassland). There is no consultative mechanism for this level of protection. The area of semi-natural land designated amounts to roughly 250,000 hectares (5.8% of the territory).

Private and State land of ecological value can also be protected by means of a Conservation Order, a stricter form of protection. Landowners are notified and are allowed to consult with the authorities. Compensation for restrictions is provided, with payments amounting to about 2,000 kroner per hectare (about £220 per hectare) in a once-off payment. On average, the compensation amounts to about 10-15% of the land value.

CONCLUSIONS

Since the 1970s, the basis for Ireland's natural habitat protection system — the proposed Natural Heritage Area designation and its predecessor (the ASI) — has been seriously hampered by lack of staff and money, no protective legislation, economic policies which have encouraged damage, and poor incentives for protection. This has resulted in a (largely unquantified) but continued degradation of Ireland's unprotected natural habitats.

Note: This chapter is based on a report by Richard Nairn commissioned for this study in 1994.

2.2

Special Protection Area (SPA)

OBJECTIVE Protection of natural habitats, fauna and flora.
LEGAL BACKING EU Directive 92/42/EEC on the conservation of natural habitats and of wild flora and fauna ('Habitats Directive'). This supersedes EU Directive 79/409/EEC on the conservation of wild birds ('Birds Directive') and the Conservation of Wild Birds Regulations (S.I. 291 of 1985).
COVERAGE 106 sites covering 205,300 ha. (1997 figures).
RESPONSIBLE AUTHORITY National Parks and Wildlife Service, Dept. of Arts, Culture and the Gaeltacht.
POWERS UNDER DESIGNATION As of 1997, powers to prevent damaging land use activities. European Commission oversees implementation in Member States and has legal powers to prevent damage or to withhold EU funds likely to damage designated sites.

BACKGROUND

Ireland's importance for birds Ireland is internationally important for its waterfowl and seabirds. Swans, geese, ducks and waders occur in internationally important numbers in winter on coastal and freshwater wetlands. Breeding waders and wildfowl occur in significant numbers on wetlands. Coastal areas and islands support breeding seabird colonies. Waterfowl and breeding seabirds can be conserved in part using protected area designations, which is the purpose of the Special Protection Area (SPA) designation.

Legal obligations under the Birds Directive
Since 1981, Ireland has been legally required to designate SPAs under the Birds Directive to protect those bird species which require habitat conservation because of their rarity or vulnerability to habitat change. Ireland is obliged to "take appropriate steps to avoid pollution or deterioration of habitats or any disturbances affecting the birds...". Designation of sites which qualify as SPAs is mandatory, and undesignated qualifying sites must be given the same protection as designated sites. Only activities which do not have significant effects on birds are permitted in SPAs. The Birds Directive also requires the avoidance of pollution or deterioration of habitats generally, outside specifically protected sites. From 1981 to 1987, the SPA was the only Irish nature designation subject to EU legal sanction.

Irish Regulations for SPAs Until 1997, the Birds Directive was implemented in Ireland through the Conservation of Wild Birds Regulations (S.I. 291 of 1985), which prohibited littering and pollution but not damaging changes in land use such as drainage, and there was no interaction with the Planning Acts. The European Commission is empowered to take *infringement proceedings* against any Member State for failing to implement the Birds Directive, in which the final outcome may be decided by the European Court of Justice. The Irish Regulations, and the designation of the first four SPAs, were drawn up in 1985 following an infringement proceeding. A further infringement proceeding was made in 1991 because the number of SPAs at that time (17) was too small and the Regulations could not legally protect habitats.

Puffin on Great Saltee Island, Co. Wexford.
Ireland has many internationally important seabird sites, especially on cliffs or offshore islands.

Oscar Merne / NPWS

TABLE 2.3 SPECIAL PROTECTION AREAS IN IRELAND (MARCH 1997 FIGURES)

		(HECTARES)	TYPE(S)	SPECIES	DESIGNATIONS
Glenveagh National Park	Donegal	9,593	lakes, bogs, woodland	waterfowl	NP
Horn Head cliffs	Donegal	176	sea cliffs	seabirds	RF
Trawbreaga Bay	Donegal	1003	sea bay	waterfowl	WS, R
Dunfanaghy	Donegal	625	lake	waterfowl	WS
Tory Island	Donegal	607	marine island	seabirds	
Lough Swilly	Donegal	3,106	sea bay	waterfowl	R
Lough Derg	Donegal	887	lake	waterfowl	
Lough Fern	Donegal	184	lake	waterfowl	
Sheskinmore Lough	Donegal	944	lagoon		
Inisbofin, Inisdooey, Inishbeg	Donegal	604	marine islands		
Lough Barra Bog	Donegal	739	blanket bog		NR
Greer's Island	Donegal	19	marine island		
Lough Foyle	Donegal	347	estuary		
Lough Nillan	Donegal	4,168	blanket bog		
Pettigoe Plateau	Donegal	691	blanket bog		NR
Inistrahull	Donegal	315	marine island		
Cummeen Strand	Sligo	1,491	estuary	waterfowl	R
Lissadell, Drumcliff	Sligo	1,575	sea bay, grassland	waterfowl	NR, WS
Lough Gara	Sligo	1,742	lake	waterfowl	R
Lough Arrow	Sligo/Roscommon	1,266	lake	waterfowl	WS
Killala Bay and River Moy estuary	Sligo/Mayo	1,061	sea bay, estuary	waterfowl	R
Inishmurray	Sligo	260	marine island	seabirds	
Lough Cullin	Mayo	1,135	lake	waterfowl	
Illanmaster	Mayo	164	marine island	seabirds	
Blacksod and Broadhaven Bays	Mayo	7,376	sea bays	seabirds	R
Inishkea Islands	Mayo	272	marine islands	waterfowl	RF
Cross Lough	Mayo	108	lake	waterfowl	
Carrowmore Lake	Mayo	966	lake	waterfowl	
Lough Carra	Mayo	1,594	lake	waterfowl	WS
Lough Conn	Mayo	5,291	lake	waterfowl	
Lough Mask	Mayo	8,529	lake	waterfowl	
Stags of Broadhaven	Mayo	136	sea cliffs	seabirds	
Inishglora and Inishkeeragh	Mayo	337	marine islands		
Termoncarragh Lake	Mayo	377	lake		
Owenduff/Nephin complex	Mayo	25,622	blanket bog		
Lough Corrib	Galway/Mayo	17,728	lake	waterfowl	R
Inner Galway Bay	Galway	11,904	sea bay, islands	seabirds, waterfowl	WS, R
Lough Scannive	Galway	49	lake		
Coole/Garryland	Galway	389	turlough		NR
Rahasane Turlough	Galway	221	turlough		
Middle Suck Callows	Galway/Roscommon	3,225	callows		
Middle Shannon Callows	Galway/Offaly/Tipperary/ Westmeath	669	callows		
Lough Derg	Galway, Tipperary, Clare	11,989	lake	waterfowl	WS, SUW
Bellangare Bog	Roscommon	1,243	raided bog		
Mutton Island	Clare	516	marine island	seabirds	
Mattle Island	Clare	53	marine island	seabirds	
Lough Cutra	Galway	387	lake	waterfowl	
High Island	Galway	169	marine island	seabirds	
Cliffs of Moher	Clare	140	sea cliffs	seabirds	RF
Ballyallia Lake	Clare	308	lake	waterfowl	R
Lough Gill	Kerry	157	lake, reedbed	waterfowl	WS
Tralee Bay	Kerry	754	sea bay, tidal lagoon	waterfowl	NR, R
Castlemaine Harbour	Kerry	2,973	sea bay, spits	waterfowl	NR, WS, R
Blasket Islands	Kerry	287	marine islands	seabirds, waterfowl	
Puffin Island	Kerry	53	marine island	seabirds	NR

		(HECTARES)	TYPE(S)	SPECIES	DESIGNATIONS
The Skelligs	Kerry	25	marine islands	seabirds	NR
Killarney National Park	Kerry	10,329	woodland, lakes, bogs	waterfowl	NP, UNBPR
Eirk Bog	Kerry	13	blanket bog		NR
Akeragh Lough	Kerry	1,199	lagoon		
Cork Harbour	Cork	1,436	sea bay, estuaries	waterfowl	R
Ballycotton	Cork	93	diverse salt/fresh water	waterfowl, seabirds	WS, R
Ballymacoda	Cork	375	estuary, marsh	waterfowl	R
Bull and Cow Rocks	Cork	336	marine rocky islands	seabirds	RF
Old Head of Kinsale	Cork	15	sea cliffs	seabirds	RF
The Gearagh	Cork	323	reservoir		NR, R. BGR
Kilcolman Bog	Cork	63	fen		NR
Blackwater Callows	Cork/Waterford	1,053	callows		
Blackwater Estuary	Cork/Waterford	468	estuary	waterfowl	R
Dungarvan Harbour	Waterford	1,041	sea bay, spit	waterfowl	R
Tramore Backstrand	Waterford	367	shallow bay	waterfowl	R
Bannow Bay	Wexford	958	sea bay	waterfowl	WS, R
Ballyteige/The Cull/Killag	Wexford	526	estuary/polder	waterfowl, seabirds	NR, BGR
Saltee Islands	Wexford	126	marine islands	seabirds	
Lady's Island Lake	Wexford	356	lagoon, islands	seabirds, waterfowl	RF
Wexford Nature Reserve	Wexford	110	polder, sea bay	waterfowl	WS
The Raven	Wexford	589	sand dunes	waterfowl	NR
Tacumshin Lake	Wexford	528	lagoon		
Wicklow National Park	Wicklow	15,399	bogs, lakes, woodland	waterfowl	NP
Poulaphouca Reservoir	Wicklow	1,949	reservoir	waterfowl	
Kilcoole Marshes	Wicklow	150	marsh		
North Bull Island	Dublin	1,395	dunes, saltmarsh, mudflat	waterfowl, seabirds	NR, R, UNBPR, SAAO, WS
Sandymount Strand/Tolka Estuary	Dublin	653	mud/sand flats	waterfowl	R
Baldoyle Bay	Dublin	203	estuary	waterfowl	NR, R
Malahide Estuary	Dublin	546	estuary	waterfowl	NR, R
Rogerstown Estuary	Dublin	195	estuary	waterfowl	NR, R, WS
Rockabill	Dublin	1	marine island	seabirds	RF
Lambay Island	Dublin	612	marine island	seabirds	
Dundalk Bay	Louth	4,767	sea bay, estuaries	waterfowl	WS, R
Carlingford Lough	Louth	172	estuary		
Stabannan-Braganstown	Louth	491	polder		
Lough Oughter	Cavan	1,463	lake	waterfowl	WS, SUW, R
Lough Sheelin	Cavan	1,885	lake	waterfowl	
Lough Ree	Ros., WMh, L'ford	10,788	lake	waterfowl	SUW
Lough Owel	Westmeath	1,032	lake	waterfowl	R
Lough Iron	Westmeath	181	lake	waterfowl	WS, R
Glen Lough	Longford, Westmeath	80	lake	waterfowl	R
Lough Ennel	Westmeath	1,403	lake	waterfowl	R
Lough Derravarragh	Westmeath	1,120	lake	waterfowl	R
Garriskill Bog	Westmeath	324	raised bog		
Lough Kinale/Derragh Lough	Ca., L'ford, WMh	280	lakes	waterfowl	
Ballykenny Fisherstown Bog	Longford	1,352	raised bog		
Mongan Bog	Offaly	127	raised bog	waterfowl	NR, BGR, WS, R
All Saints Bog	Offaly	326	raised bog		NR
Little Brosna Callows	Offaly	1,154	callows		

Abbreviations

NR: Nature Reserve
R: Ramsar Site
BGR: Biogenetic Reserve
RF: Refuge for Fauna

UNBPR: Unesco Biosphere Reserve
WS: Wildfowl Sanctuary
TPO: Tree Preservation Order
SUW: Sensitive Area for Urban Wastewater

SAAO: Special Amenity Area Order
Source: National Parks and Wildlife Service

23

Table 2.4   The percentage of some groups and species of birds which would be protected by the proposed network of SPAs

SPECIES	ANNEX 1 OF BIRDS DIRECTIVE	TOTAL POPULATION	% IN PROPOSED SPAS
Breeding seabirds	some	420,000 pairs	72
Roseate Tern	yes	422 pairs	100
Little tern	yes	390 pairs	62
Wintering waders	some	870,000 individuals	50
Golden plover	yes	200,000 individuals	48
Wintering wildfowl	some	440,000 individuals	74
Whooper swan	yes	10,320 individuals	69
Greenland white-fronted goose	yes	14,000 individuals	76
Peregrine falcon	yes	300 pairs	2
Corncrake	yes	less than 300 males	20
Chough	yes	671 pairs	0.7

Source: JNCC Report (Way et al, 1993).
Note: Annex 1 species are listed in the EU Birds Directive as requiring *special habitat conservation measures*.

SPA designation programme in Ireland

From 1985 to 1991, 20 SPAs covering 6,959 ha. were designated; all were coastal areas and uninhabited islands, 80% of which were on State-owned land and foreshore. Following the second infringement proceeding in 1991, the National Parks and Wildlife Service (NPWS) began to designate 56 sites recommended in an independent report which it commissioned jointly with the Department of Environment in Northern Ireland. A substantial number of sites were designated in the past several years: in 1996, 75 sites became SPAs, increasing to 106 sites in 1997, with a further 13 proposed for designation by April 1997. The European Commission also demanded stricter national legislation, which is now addressed by the Natural Habitats Regulations. Table 2.4 shows the proportions of some groups and species of birds which would be protected by the recommended network of 56 SPAs. Breeding seabirds and wintering waterfowl fare relatively well. Dispersed species fare poorly, and wider countryside measures are needed for their protection (Way *et al.*, 1993).

The designation programme is now almost complete and SPAs cover about 200,000 ha. or nearly 3% of the territory. Most of the sites are estuaries, coastal bays and inlets, offshore islands and inland lakes. At least 90% of this area is State-owned foreshore, inland lakes, Nature Reserves and National Parks. These are listed in Table 2.5 of the first edition; Clonakilty Bay is still the subject of a court case and has not yet been designated. Designation of SPAs is facilitated since the introduction of the European Habitats Regulations in February 1997 (see Section 2.3), since all SPAs are being incorporated in the network of SACs (Natura 2000), which have a formal designation procedure.

SPA designation procedure Sites proposed for designation are first advertised and the public are allowed time for comments/objections, which may be taken into account by the NPWS. Since 1991, the boundaries of SPAs have largely been determined by ownership rather than by ecological criteria. State-owned areas have been designated, while some non State-owned sections of qualifying sites have not yet been included. This practice is aimed at speeding up the process of site designation. Eventually, privately owned land will be included, and site boundaries are expected to follow the NHA boundaries.

EVALUATION

Management in SPAs Few SPAs have been actively managed. Wexford Wildfowl Reserve, Rockabill and Lady's Island Lake are managed for their birds, but these are managed under other designations. However, this situation may

25

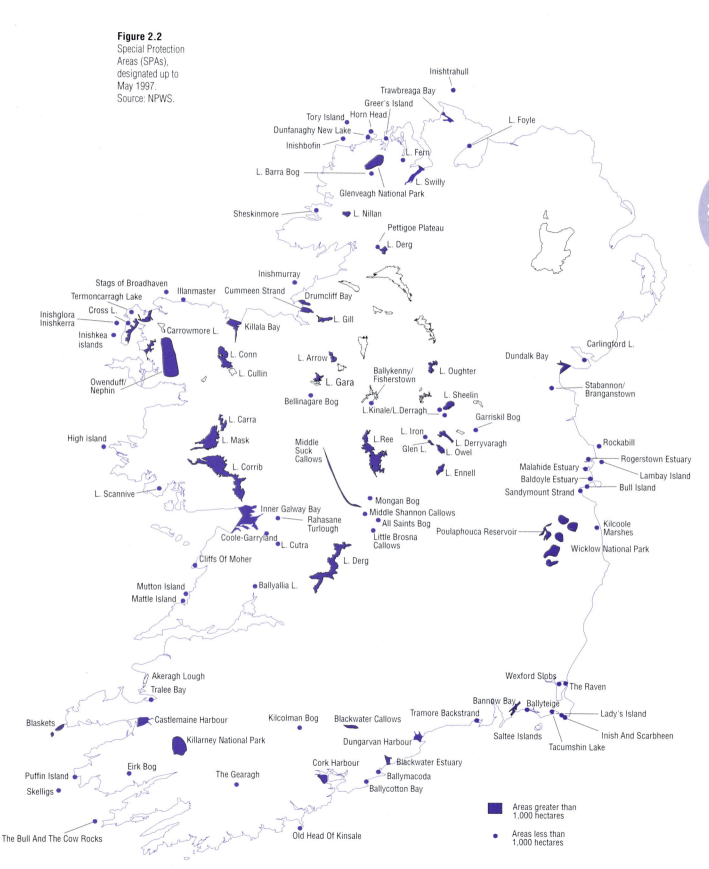

Figure 2.2
Special Protection
Areas (SPAs),
designated up to
May 1997.
Source: NPWS.

Inishtrahull

Trawbreaga Bay

Greer's Island

Horn Head

Tory Island

Dunfanaghy New Lake

Inishbofin

L. Foyle

L. Fern

L. Barra Bog

L. Swilly

Glenveagh National Park

Sheskinmore

L. Nillan

Pettigoe Plateau

L. Derg

Inishmurray

Stags of Broadhaven

Illanmaster

Cummeen Strand

Drumcliff Bay

Termoncarragh Lake

Cross L.

L. Gill

Inishglora
Inishkerra

Carrowmore L.

Killala Bay

Carlingford L.

Inishkea
islands

L. Conn

L. Arrow

Dundalk Bay

Ballykenny/
Fisherstown

L. Oughter

Stabannon/
Branganstown

Owenduff/
Nephin

L. Cullin

L. Gara

L. Sheelin

Bellinagare Bog

L.Kinale/L.Derragh

Garriskil Bog

L. Carra

L. Mask

Middle
Suck
Callows

L.Ree

L. Iron

L. Derryvaragh

Rockabill

High Island

Glen L.

L. Owel

Rogerstown Estuary

L. Corrib

L. Ennell

Malahide Estuary

Lambay Island

L. Scannive

Baldoyle Estuary

Bull Island

Sandymount Strand

Inner Galway Bay

Mongan Bog

Rahasane
Turlough

Middle Shannon Callows

All Saints Bog

Coole-Garryland

L. Cutra

Little Brosna
Callows

Poulaphouca Reservoir

Kilcoole
Marshes

Cliffs Of Moher

L. Derg

Wicklow National Park

Mutton Island
Mattle Island

Ballyallia L.

Akeragh Lough

Tralee Bay

Wexford Slobs

The Raven

Bannow Bay

Ballyteige

Lady's Island

Blaskets

Castlemaine Harbour

Kilcolman Bog

Blackwater Callows

Tramore Backstrand

Killarney National Park

Dungarvan Harbour

Saltee Islands

Inish And Scarbheen

Tacumshin Lake

Puffin Island

Eirk Bog

The Gearagh

Cork Harbour

Blackwater Estuary

Ballymacoda

Skelligs

Ballycotton Bay

The Bull And The Cow Rocks

Old Head Of Kinsale

Areas greater than
1,000 hectares

Areas less than
1,000 hectares

now change. The Natural Habitats Regulations, 1997 provide for management of all such designated sites, and the Regulations cover SPAs.

Threats to designated sites The current network of designated SPAs consists of coastal areas (marine cliffs, offshore islands, mudflats and sandflats) and inland lakes, which are not subject to the range of pressures and threats of land-based sites. As the SPA network expands to inland sites, additional threats and potential conflicts will undoubtedly arise.

Potential conflict between SPAs and other policies

(i) Aquaculture: Many SPAs are estuaries or tidal bays which are also suitable for shellfish farming. The main potential impacts on SPAs are the loss of feeding area, effects on food supply, and disturbance (O'Briain, 1993). The Department of the Marine informally consults the National Parks and Wildlife Service (NPWS) about new applications for shellfish farms. Some applications were refused because of potential conflict with conservation interests (e.g. in areas of Dungarvan Harbour which are known to be important for waterfowl). Fish farms have been permitted in zones which are marginal for waterfowl.

(ii) Hunting: The Birds Directive specifies which species may be hunted, by what general means, and whether they may be sold as game. Hunting is controlled by the NPWS, and on State-owned foreshore is permitted by means of foreshore licences. Such licences are granted both within SPAs and proposed SPAs, and in other areas of foreshore which do not qualify under Article 4 of the Birds Directive. Controlled hunting is not necessarily inconsistent with SPAs, although it results in disturbance. No assessment of the impact of shooting on birds in SPAs has been made, so it is not known whether the network of Wildfowl Sanctuaries (where shooting is prohibited; see Section 2.7) is adequate. Currently, 17 SPAs are covered partly or wholly by Wildfowl Sanctuary designations.

CONCLUSIONS

Assessment of the SPA designation is difficult, since no SPA has been managed as an SPA, and most designated sites are State-owned foreshore and lakes, Nature Reserves or National Parks, none of which are subject the normal range of development threats. Hunting and aquaculture interests have made some objections to SPA designations. Until 1997, SPAs had no effective protection against habitat damage, although the Birds Directive has always provided for powerful safeguards against such damage. However, since all SPAs are now legally protected under the Natural Habitats Regulations, 1997, sites threatened by development are expected to receive some effective safeguards under Irish law.

Note: This chapter is based on a report by Eleanor Mayes commissioned for this study in 1995.

2.3

Special Area of Conservation (SAC)

OBJECTIVE Protection of natural habitats of EU importance.
LEGAL BACKING European Communities (Natural Habitats) Regulations, 1997 (S.I. No. 94 of 1997). EU Directive 92/43/EEC on the conservation of natural habitats and of wild flora and fauna.
COVERAGE Protection of natural habitats of EU importance in Ireland; roughly 551,000 ha.; approx. 400 sites.
RESPONSIBLE AUTHORITY National Parks and Wildlife Service, Dept. of Arts, Culture and the Gaeltacht; European Commission oversees implementation in EU Member States.
PROTECTIVE MEASURES Prevention of any damaging land uses on State-owned and private land.

BACKGROUND TO THE EU HABITATS DIRECTIVE

Modern developments have seriously encroached on Europe's remaining natural areas, especially in the last three decades. The main aim of the Habitats Directive is to conserve the best examples of natural and semi-natural habitats and species of flora and fauna throughout the EU. Each Member State is required to designate Special Areas of Conservation (SACs) to protect those habitats and species which are listed in the annexes of the Directive.

The EU intends to create a network of designated areas throughout the Community, entitled Natura 2000. Each SAC must be given sufficient protection so as to conserve adequately the listed habitats and/or species. A number of 'priority' habitats are listed which deserve special attention (e.g. peatlands and sand dunes in Ireland), and EU funds can be used to assist in their conservation. Stricter protection is given in the Directive to SACs which have priority habitats and species.

THE NATURAL HABITATS REGULATIONS, 1997 (S.I. NO. 94 OF 1997)

Prior to the introduction of the Natural Habitats Regulations, only habitats within Nature Reserves and National Parks stood a reasonable chance of being protected. Restriction in the use of private land has always been unpopular with the strong rural lobby. The inclusion of payments to landowners was politically crucial for the Regulations to be passed.

The transposition of the Habitats Directive into Irish law on 26 February 1997, represents a fundamental shift in nature conservation policy in Ireland. SACs will account for about two-thirds of all the recognised natural areas. The remaining sites, identified as Natural Heritage Areas (NHAs) accounting for approximately 150,000 ha., do not come under the protection of the Natural Habitats Regulations, and will only be afforded limited legal protections when the Wildlife Act, 1976 is amended. From 1997, extensive areas of private and State land (see Figure 2.3) are expected to have legal protection against damaging developments and some sites may also be subject to positive conservation measures. Four hundred candidate sites have been listed by the National Parks and Wildlife Service (NPWS).

The list of candidate sites drawn up by the National Parks and Wildlife Service is required to be sent to the European Commission, which has the power to adopt or reject a site as an SAC, based on scientific evidence. Designation has to be made within six years of adoption by the Commission, but is expected to be completed within several years. The first list of candidate SACs was published in March 1997.

PROVISIONS FOR CONSERVATION IN SPECIAL AREAS OF CONSERVATION

Legal provisions for conservation in SACs include the following:

– permission for damaging developments in non-priority habitats may only be given for imperative reasons of overriding public interest;
– permission for damaging developments in

Figure 2.3
Candidate SACs. Note the considerable overlap with NHAs (Figure 2.1). Source: NPWS. (Reproduced by kind permission of the Minister for Arts, Culture and the Gaeltacht.)

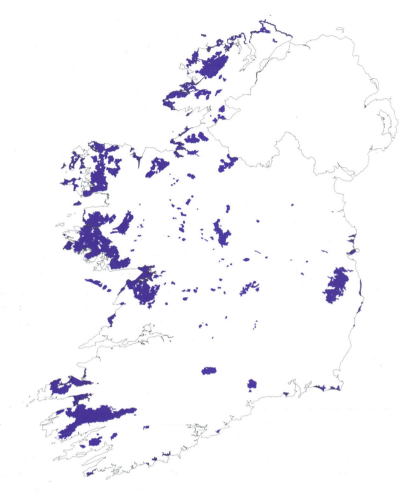

'priority' habitats (e.g. designated peatlands, sand dunes, limestone pavement, turloughs) may only be given for overriding health and safety reasons;

— there must be assessment of developments not connected with, or which take place outside an SAC, but which might have a significant impact on it;

— sites damaged illegally must be restored;

— local authorities must assess developments prior to making decisions on planning applications;

— landowners must be notified of designations;

— landowners may be compensated for proven loss of income arising from designation;

— management agreements may be made with landowners;

— management plans should be prepared, either for specific sites or integrated into Development Plans.

Assessment of the effectiveness of the SAC designation will only be possible towards the end of the century, when most sites are expected to be designated. Even though the most important natural sites in Ireland will be designated as SACs, this does not in itself guarantee their effective conservation (see Overall Conclusions: Nature Designations, page 50).

IMPLEMENTATION

How effective are the Natural Habitats Regulations? It is likely that the outcome of specific cases will determine their effectiveness in practice. The Minister is given the powers to decide if a development should proceed in an SAC if for "overriding health and safety reasons" or for "imperative reasons of overriding public interest". Some large scale developments such as sewage treatment plants, roads and landfill sites, for example, could prove controversial, depending on the Minister's interpretation of the regulations.

2.4

Statutory Nature Reserve

OBJECTIVE Strict protection of natural habitats, fauna and flora.
LEGAL BACKING Wildlife Act, 1976.
COVERAGE 0.26 % of the territory; 78 sites covering 18,095 ha.
RESPONSIBLE AUTHORITY National Parks and Wildlife Service, Dept. of Arts, Culture and the Gaeltacht.
POWERS UNDER DESIGNATION Powers of strict protection of flora, fauna and habitats on State or private land; making of management agreements with landowners.

BACKGROUND

Statutory Nature Reserves are regarded as the most rigorous mechanism in Ireland for the protection of ecosystems and species of fauna and flora. Ireland's Statutory Nature Reserve network is still very small and has been in existence only since 1980. Most Nature Reserves are in State ownership. All Nature Reserves are NHAs (see page 15), and a proportion of reserves will be designated as SACs (see page 27).

LEGISLATION

Almost all damaging activities can be legally prevented in Nature Reserves. The 1976 Wildlife Act empowers the NPWS to designate Nature Reserves on State or private land for habitats of plants and animals or habitats of scientific interest. There is an obligation to manage the land designated in accordance with the objectives for which it is designated. Government departments and State companies which are involved in activities that may affect a reserve are required to consult with the NPWS and to take all practicable steps to avoid or minimise any potential damage.

NATURE RESERVE ACQUISITION PROGRAMME

A total of 78 areas were designated as Nature Reserves in 1995, covering 18,095 ha. (see Table 2.6 and Figure 2.4). Other overlapping designations are also indicated. The main habitats represented in 74 Nature Reserves and the size range of sites are given in Table 2.7. A certain amount of undesignated land has been acquired for Nature Reserves, especially peatlands, which is not shown in the tables.

Woodlands, peatlands and intertidal areas are the best represented, while very few grasslands,

sand dunes, marine sites or fens are protected. EU policy has influenced Nature Reserve acquisition. The proportion of reserves which include 'priority' habitats (as defined in the Habitats Directive; see page 27) has increased from 19% of Reserves designated between 1980 and 1984, to 86% of Reserves designated between 1990 and 1994. Ireland's Nature Reserve network is small in European terms, representing only 0.26% of the country. In comparison, Nature Reserves in Scotland occupy 1.4%, England 0.4%, Wales 0.6% and Northern Ireland 0.3%, respectively. In recent years, considerable progress has been made in acquiring peatlands for conservation (see box).

Ownership of Nature Reserves prior to establishment In only a few cases the State bore the purchase cost for an entire site from private ownership, such as Slieve Carron, Lissadell and Lough Barra Bog. Forty-nine Reserves were originally acquired by the State for afforestation, peat extraction or other activities that would have damaged the conservation value of the sites.

EVALUATION

A detailed survey was made of 21 Nature Reserves, together with summary information on the remainder.

Management objectives for Nature Reserves Management needs are based on existing knowledge of sites and availability of staff and resources. These are set out in a conservation report or schedule. For example, in Knocksink Wood, objectives are removal of conifers and the control of amenity use; in Ballyteige Burrow, the objectives are to control grazing and damaging leisure activities, and to prevent pollution and dumping. Management plans

Table 2.6 Statutory Nature Reserves

NATURE RSERVE	COUNTY	DATE	AREA (HA.)	MAIN HABITATS (* = PRIORITY, EU HABITATS DIRECTIVE)	SPECIAL INTEREST	OVERLAPPING DESIGNATIONS	PREVIOUS OWNERSHIP
Derryclare	Galway	1980	19	Woodland			State forestry
Glen of the Downs	Wicklow	1980	59	Woodland			State forestry
Ballykeeffe	Kilkenny	1980	55	Woodland			State forestry
Garryricken	Kilkenny	1980	28	Woodland			State forestry
Kyleadohir	Kilkenny	1980	59	Woodland			State forestry
Cahermurphy	Clare	1980	9	Woodland			State forestry
Wexford Wildfowl Reserve	Wexford	1981	194	Grassland	Waterfowl	SPA, R, BGR	PPC
Lough Hyne	Cork	1981	65	Marine inlet		BGR	State foreshore
Uragh Wood	Kerry	1981	87	Woodland			State forestry
Deputy's Pass	Wicklow	1982	47	Woodland			State forestry
Grantstown Wood/Lough	Laois	1982	49	Woodland			State forestry
Coolacurragh Wood	Laois	1982	8	Woodland			State forestry
The Raven foreshore	Wexford	1983	589	Sand dunes*, sand flats, forestry	Waterfowl, flora	SPA, R	State forestry+
Vale of Clara	Wicklow	1983	221	Woodland			State forestry
Rosturra Wood	Galway	1983	18	Woodland			State forestry
Derrycrag Wood	Galway	1983	110	Woodland			State forestry
Ballynastaig Wood	Galway	1983	10	Woodland			State forestry
Coole-Garryland	Galway	1983	364	Woodland, turlough*, lake, limestone pavement*			State forestry
Pollnaknockaun	Galway	1983	39	Woodland			State forestry
Oldhead Wood	Mayo	1984	17	Woodland			State forestry
Pettigo Plateau	Donegal	1984	900	Blanket bog*, lake, flushes	Waterfowl	R, BGR	State forestry
Dromore	Clare	1985	370	Woodland, limestone pavement*, fen, grassland, lake	Waterfowl		State forestry
Richmond Esker	Galway	1985	16	Woodland, grassland			State forestry
Timahoe Esker	Laois	1985	13	Woodland, grassland			State forestry
Slieve Bloom Mountains	Laois/Offaly	1985	2300	Blanket bog*	Raptors	R, BGR	State forestry
Capel Island/Knockadoon	Cork	1985	161	Island cliff			†Private
Capel Island marine	Cork	1985	127	Sub-littoral			State foreshore
Keelahilla, Slieve Carron	Clare	1986	145	Limestone pavement*, grassland, woodland		BGR	PPC
Duntally Wood	Donegal	1986	15	Woodland			State forestry
Rathmullan Wood	Donegal	1986	33	Woodland		TPO	State forestry
Ballyarr Wood	Donegal	1986	30	Woodland			State forestry
Knockmoyle/Sheskin	Mayo	1986	732	Blanket bog*		R, BGR	State forestry/Bord na Móna
Mount Brandon	Kerry	1986	462	Blanket bog*, cliffs	Flora		State forestry
Pollardstown Fen	Kildare	1986	130	Fen*, tufa spring*		R, BGR	State forestry/Bord na Móna
Eirk Bog	Kerry	1986	16	Transition bog*	Waterfowl, raptors		State forestry
Balgigan, Lissadell	Sligo	1986	29	Grassland	Waterfowl		PPC
Owenboy	Mayo	1986	397	Blanket bog*	Waterfowl	R, BGR	State forestry
Ballyteige	Clare	1986	6	Grassland, heath, flushes, scrub			State forestry
Clara Bog	Offaly	1987	460	Raised bog*		R, BGR	Bord na Móna
Lough Barra Bog	Donegal	1987	176	Blanket bog*, pools, flushes, woodland	Waterfowl	R	PPC
Puffin Island	Kerry	1987	54	Island cliffs	Breeding seabirds	SPA	†IWC
Puffin Island marine	Kerry	1987	34	Sub-littoral			State foreshore
Mongan Bog	Offaly	1987	119	Raised bog*		R, BGR	†An Taisce

Name	County	Year	Area (ha)	Habitat	Species/Interest	Designations	Ownership
The Gearagh	Cork	1987	300	Wet woodland		R, BGR	†ESB
Raheenmore Bog	Offaly	1987	162	Raised bog*		BGR	Bord na Móna
Ballyteige Burrow	Wexford	1987	539	Sand dunes*, heath, mudflat	Waterfowl, flora	SPA, BGR	PPC/State foreshore
Glendalough	Wicklow	1988	157	Woodland		NP	State forestry
Glenealo Valley	Wicklow	1988	1958	Blanket bog*, heath	Raptors	NP	State forestry
Lough Yganavan	Kerry	1988	25	Lake	Natterjack toad		State forestry
Lough Nambrackdarrig	Kerry	1988	4	Lake	Natterjack toad		State forestry
Derkmore Wood	Donegal	1988	7	Woodland			State forestry
Rogerstown Estuary	Dublin	1988	195	Mud and sand flats	Waterfowl	SPA, R	State foreshore
North Bull Island	Dublin	1988	118	Sand dunes*, salt marsh	Waterfowl, flora	SPA, R, UNBPR	†Dublin Corporation
North Bull Island shore	Dublin	1988	1318	Mud and sand flats	Waterfowl	SPA, R, UNBPR	State foreshore
Baldoyle Estuary	Dublin	1988	203	Mud and sand flats, saltmarsh	Waterfowl	SPA, R	State
Fiddown Island	Kilkenny	1988	63	Reedswamp, scrub			PPC
Great Skellig	Kerry	1988	23	Island cliffs	Breeding seabirds		State
Little Skellig	Kerry	1988	8	Island cliffs	Breeding seabirds		†IWC
Tralee Bay	Kerry	1989	755	Mudflats	Waterfowl	SPA, R	State forestry
Derrymore Island	Kerry	1989	106	Sand dunes*, saltmarsh			†Private
Tearaght Island	Kerry	1989	27	Island cliffs	Breeding seabirds	SPA	†Irish Lights
Tearaght Island marine	Kerry	1989	19	Sub-littoral			State foreshore
Knockomagh Wood	Cork	1989	12	Woodland			State forestry
Derrycunihy Wood	Kerry	1989	136	Woodland, bog, lakeshore			State forestry
Easkey Bog	Sligo	1990	607	Blanket bog*			State forestry
Knockmoyle/Sheskin	Mayo	1990	466	Blanket bog*	Waterfowl	R	Bord na Móna
Sheheree Bog	Kerry	1990	9	Raised bog*		R, BGR	†Private
Castlemaine Harbour	Kerry	1990	927	Mud and sand flats	Waterfowl	R	State foreshore
Ballyteige Burrow	Wexford	1990	8	Saltmarsh	Flora	R	PPC
Meenachullion	Donegal	1990	194	Blanket bog*	Waterfowl, raptors		State forestry
Glengarriff Wood	Cork	1991	301	Woodland			State forestry
Leam West Bog	Galway	1991	373	Blanket bog*			State forestry
Redwood Bog	Tipperary	1991	132	Raised bog*	Waterfowl		Bord na Móna
Scragh Bog	Westmeath	1992	23	Fen	Flora		PPC (gift), State forestry
Kilcolman Bog	Cork	1994	21	Fen, lake	Waterfowl		†Kilcolman Wildfowl Reserve
Kilcolman Bog	Cork	1994	30	Fen, lake	Waterfowl		LC/private
Cummeragh River Bog	Kerry	1994	45	Transition bog*			PPC (gift)
Knocksink Wood	Wicklow	1994	52	Woodland			State forestry

Source: National Parks and Wildlife Service

31

Abbreviations

*: Priority Habitats under the EU Habitats Directive
SPA: Special Protection Area under EU Birds Directive
R: Ramsar Site
BGR: Biogenetic Reserve
UNBPR: Unesco Biosphere Reserve
PPC: land purchased from private ownership

PPC (gift): purchased by the Dutch Society for the Conservation of Irish Bogs and the Irish Peatland Conservation Council and gifted to the State
LC: Land Commission
†: Section 16 Nature Reserves which may be owned privately, by voluntary bodies or other bodies
TPO: Tree Protection Order
IWC: Irish Wildbird Conservancy

Figure 2.4
Distribution of Nature Reserves in the
Republic of Ireland. Note the absence of
reserves in eleven counties. Ten
reserves exceed 500 ha.; thirty-eight
reserves are less than 100 ha.
(Source: NPWS.)

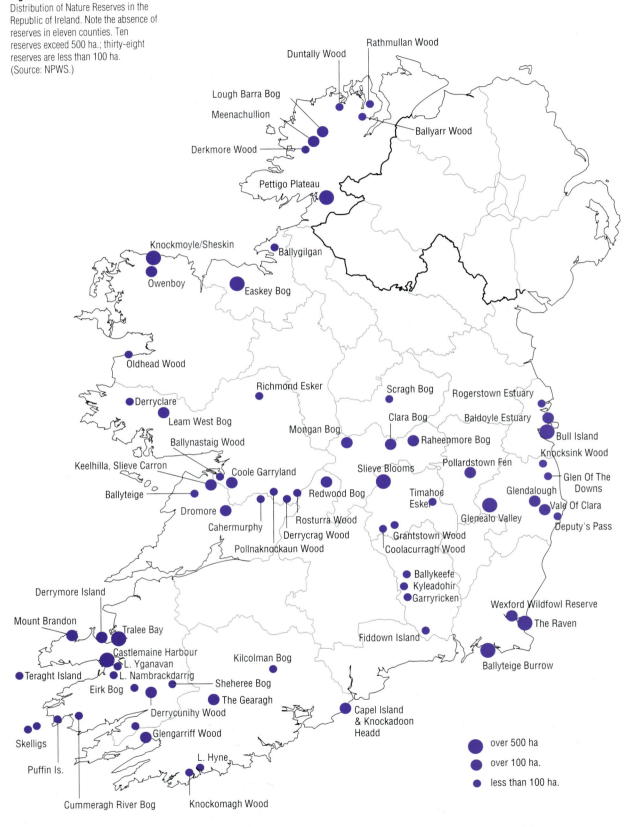

Rathmullan Wood
Duntally Wood
Lough Barra Bog
Meenachullion
Ballyarr Wood
Derkmore Wood
Pettigo Plateau
Knockmoyle/Sheskin
Ballygilgan
Owenboy
Easkey Bog
Oldhead Wood
Richmond Esker
Scragh Bog
Rogerstown Estuary
Derryclare
Clara Bog
Baldoyle Estuary
Leam West Bog
Bull Island
Mongan Bog
Raheenmore Bog
Knocksink Wood
Ballynastaig Wood
Pollardstown Fen
Keelhilla, Slieve Carron
Coole Garryland
Slieve Blooms
Glen Of The Downs
Ballyteige
Redwood Bog
Glendalough
Dromore
Timahoe Esker
Vale Of Clara
Cahermurphy
Rosturra Wood
Glenealo Valley
Derrycrag Wood
Deputy's Pass
Pollnaknockaun Wood
Grantstown Wood
Coolacurragh Wood
Ballykeefe
Kyleadohir
Garryricken
Wexford Wildfowl Reserve
Derrymore Island
The Raven
Mount Brandon
Tralee Bay
Fiddown Island
Castlemaine Harbour
Kilcolman Bog
Ballyteige Burrow
L. Yganavan
Teraght Island
L. Nambrackdarrig
Sheheree Bog
Eirk Bog
The Gearagh
Capel Island & Knockadoon Headd
Derrycunihy Wood
Skelligs
Glengarriff Wood
Puffin Is.
L. Hyne
Cummeragh River Bog
Knockomagh Wood

over 500 ha
over 100 ha.
less than 100 ha.

Table 2.7   The main habitats represented in 74 Nature Reserves

HABITAT TYPE	SIZE RANGE (HECTARES)	MEAN AREA (HECTARES)	TOTAL AREA (HECTARES)	NUMBER OF SITES PROTECTED
Woodland	7-370	90	2,786	31
Blanket bog	176-2,300	857	8,568	10
Transition bog	16-45	31	61	2
Raised bog	9-460	176	880	5
Fen	23-130	68	204	3
Grassland	6-194	76	228	3
Marine island/cliff	8-161	55	275	5
Marine/sub-littoral	19-127	61	244	4
Sand dunes/intertidal mud and sand flats	106-1,318	528	4,758	8
Lake	4-25	15	30	2
Reedswamp		63	63	1
TOTAL			**18,097**	**74**

have been made for some Reserves, but there is no specific requirement for management plans, guidelines for their content, or audits, and there is no procedure to ensure that management prescriptions are carried out.

Damage to Nature Reserves Damage to Nature Reserves is difficult to assess, as there is no formal monitoring. Staff may visit a site as seldom as once a year. Ten (48%) out of the 21 Reserves examined have no management records. Of the 11 Reserves with management records, 8 are known to have been damaged since they were designated (damage included turf cutting, overgrazing and recreational use).

Damage prevention in Nature Reserves State ownership of Nature Reserves does not by itself prevent damage occurring. Incursion by farm animals, turbary, and theft of timber are the most common causes. Persistent offenders are prosecuted under civil law, and injunctions have also been sought to prevent damage to Nature Reserves. The Wildlife Act provides for the making of regulations governing public access and activities within Nature Reserves, but due to a technical difficulty with the Act (Section 59), regulations have not been produced. Grazing agreements, where appropriate, are sought for grassland and blanket bog Reserves. Where grazing is causing damage, adjustments are made to the stocking levels, mowing or control of exotic species.

Resources for management of Nature Reserves With the exception of a handful of sites, there are no wardens assigned exclusively to monitor and manage Nature Reserves. In comparison, the Royal Society for the Protection of Birds, a voluntary conservation organisation in the UK, manages 120 reserves totalling 76,000 ha, about half of which it owns, the rest being subject to management agreements. The RSPB employs 16 executive staff, over 100 site-based employees including wardens, stockmen and farm managers, and up to 100 temporary wardens. A similar ratio of staff to area protected would give the NPWS about 50 staff working exclusively in reserve management.

Glengarrif Wood Nature Reserve, Co. Cork. Only tiny fragments of native woodland remain. Many are now protected in Nature Reserves and National Parks.

NPWS

The North Slob, Co. Wexford, Nature Reserve for wintering Greenland White-fronted Geese. Drainage of wetland sites throughout Ireland has made this site of special importance, as large numbers of geese migrate here annually.

IRELAND'S PEATLAND ACQUISITION PROGRAMME

Peatlands have disappeared at an alarming rate in Europe. Virtually all natural peatlands have been lost in the Netherlands, Germany and Poland. In the United Kingdom, 98% of raised bogs and 90% of blanket bogs have been lost. In Ireland, where it was assumed there were abundant areas of peatland covering one sixth of the country, 94% of raised bogs and 86% of blanket bogs have been damaged or destroyed. Less than 112,000 ha. of blanket bog and 18,000 ha. of raised bog survive relatively intact. The Irish Government in 1990 committed itself to an acquisition target of 10,000 ha. of raised bogs and 40,000 ha of blanket bogs. By 1992, the State had acquired 40% of its blanket bog target and 22% of its raised bog target. By 1996, the State had protected nearly 70% (27,642 ha.) of its blanket bog target and over 30% (3,091 ha.) of its raised bog target. Protected fens (transition phase in bog development) account for 353 ha. The total area of peatlands designated or awaiting designation as Nature Reserves and in National Parks amounts to 31,086 ha. (IPCC, 1996).

Con O'Rourke

occurring; its extent is unknown, but observation of a number of sites suggests that in most cases, damage is slight. Management staff numbers are inadequate. The rate of site designation has declined substantially in recent years. Since about 1990, EU funding for acquisition of 'priority' habitats (see Section 2.3) has dictated the types of habitats acquired.

Nevertheless, although the situation is unsatisfactory, the Nature Reserve designation has enabled protection of a large number of small sites which would otherwise have been afforested, drained for peat extraction or agriculture. This is especially the case for peatlands.

Note: This chapter is based on a report by Eleanor Mayes commissioned for this study.

CONCLUSIONS

Many reserves are too small to effectively conserve an entire area of conservation interest. There are no more than a handful of reserves over 1,000 hectares. Over 60 reserves are less than 250 hectares. The overall network (covering over 18,000 ha.) is not yet sufficiently extensive to conserve an adequate representative sample of Irish wildlife habitats. This is not a new observation; it has been recognised for many years, and has been stated many times. Peatlands and native woods are the best represented, while there are very few protected soft coastal sites and grasslands.

Detailed baseline information and monitoring of Nature Reserves is lacking. Some damage is

National Park

OBJECTIVE Protection of ecosystems and landscapes of special importance and to provide for public use and appreciation.
LEGAL BACKING None, except for Killarney (Bourn Vincent Memorial Park Act, 1936). The anticipated National Parks and Protected Areas Bill will give sufficient legal powers to the State for control over National Parks.
COVERAGE Five parks covering 47,287 ha.; almost entirely State-owned.
RESPONSIBLE AUTHORITY National Parks and Wildlife Service, Dept. of Arts, Culture and the Gaeltacht.
POWERS UNDER DESIGNATION Prevention of any damaging land uses by virtue of ownership by the National Parks and Wildlife Service.

BACKGROUND

The twin aims of National Parks are nature conservation and public recreation and appreciation, and their tourist value is well recognised. Many, but not all National Parks in other countries are state-owned. Unlike some continental European countries, which have a longer tradition of conservation and larger areas within national parks, Ireland's parks are small and resemble large estates or nature reserves.

The five National Parks in Killarney, Connemara, Glenveagh, the Burren and Wicklow Mountains are part of a network of national parks established throughout Europe and the world. Killarney National Park is the oldest, established in 1932. Apart from Killarney, the four other parks have been established since the 1980s (see page 36).

DEVELOPMENT OF THE NATIONAL PARK NETWORK

Killarney and Glenveagh National Parks were acquired by the State as well-established estates, although both have since expanded from their original boundaries. The other parks — Connemara, Burren and Wicklow — are developing from a small nucleus (see Table 2.8).

Land acquisition policy Funding for land purchase has always been limited. There was no specific policy on land acquisition until circa 1990. EU Funds are now available to the State on a 75%: 25% basis for purchase of 'priority' habitats under the Habitats Directive (see page 27). These are peatlands, karst limestone, sand dunes and turloughs. There is also a national policy on peatland acquisition, which coincides with the EU policy. Thus, land acquisition policy for National Parks is dictated to a large extent by the EU Habitats Directive and availability of EU funds.

Land acquisition targets The target area for the Burren National Park is 3,000 ha. Wicklow National Park has an ambitious target of about 30,000 ha., all in the Wicklow uplands. Land leased from An Taisce (2,000 ha.) and other land recently acquired will greatly expand Glenveagh National Park. It is hoped to acquire some of the Roundstone blanket bog complex to the south of Connemara National Park. There are no plans for expansion of Killarney National Park. Approximately 5,000 ha. in the Owenduff/Nephin area have been acquired, which may form the core of a new National Park in north Mayo.

Table 2.8	Progress in land acquisition for National Parks				
LOCATION	**1933**	**1972-1982**	**1983**	**1995**	**1997**
Killarney	4,272	3,766	8,038	10,129	10,289
Glenveagh	—	9,667	9,667	12,343	16.548
Connemara	—	2,699	2,699	2,699	2,957
Burren	—	410	410	1,562	1,580
Wicklow Mountains	—	—	—	12,211	15,913
TOTAL	**4,272**	**16,542**	**20,814**	**38,944**	**47,287**

Source: Craig, A. (1984), National Parks and Wildlife Service, personal communication

National Parks

Glenveagh
Co. Donegal

NPWS

Connemara,
Co. Galway

NPWS

Burren,
Co. Clare

Emer Colleran

Wicklow
Mountains

David Hickie

Killarney
Co. Kerry

Ireland currently has five National
Parks covering almost 47,287
hectares. A sixth park is proposed
for North Mayo. Irish National Parks
are small by international standards.

36

RESOURCES FOR NATIONAL PARKS

While resources for management are modest, they have always been more substantial than for Nature Reserves. National Parks provide a focus for holiday makers, who spend money in surrounding areas, and thereby boost the local economy. According to Bord Fáilte, the vast majority of overseas visitors to Ireland come to enjoy the natural environment. Thus, allocating resources for National Parks is seen by politicians as an investment in tourism. In general, resources are seen as adequate for the present, with the exception that more staff are needed for research and education.

MANAGEMENT IN NATIONAL PARKS

Visitor management   There is no stated policy on visitor limitations, mainly because the problem has not yet arisen, and may not arise. There are signs of levelling off of visitor numbers in Glenveagh National Park. There is potential to limit numbers if necessary, e.g., guided tours to Glenveagh Castle have a limit of 60,000 people per year. Visitors to the castle may have to wait if there are crowds and therefore will tend to go elsewhere next time, and the car park may also limit numbers. Visitor pressure in some other National Parks is

intense, for example in the United States and Canada. Each of the 13 National Parks in England and Wales (which are essentially protected landscapes) receive visitors in their millions each year.

Habitat management   In general, habitats within all the National Parks were observed to be well managed. Management is focused on conservation of fauna and flora; farming, forestry and extractive industries are either not practised or are being phased out; there appear to be adequate numbers of staff; and the parks are in sympathetic ownership. Resources and staff are not a limiting factor in habitat management. For example, woodland regeneration in Killarney is more a political problem of controlling sheep which stray into the park from neighbouring lands. *Rhododendron ponticum* (an invasive species which suppresses native vegetation) is beginning to come under control in Glenveagh, while in Killarney, because of the much larger area affected, progress is not so advanced. Turbary (traditional turf cutting) is reported as not being a problem. It would be unusual if some management problems were not encountered. Some examples are illustrated (see box below).

SHEEP GRAZING: AN EXAMPLE OF A MANAGEMENT PROBLEM IN IRISH NATIONAL PARKS

Currently, EU sheep subsidies have encouraged farmers to expand flocks to levels which far exceed the grazing capacity of the land, especially on the western seaboard. At first, sheep allowed to persistently stray into the Connemara National Park were impounded, which is unpopular locally. Subsequently, a sheep fence, proposed by an adjoining landowner and agreed with the parks staff, was granted permission by Galway Co. Council but refused by An Bord Pleanála on the grounds that it would interfere with scenic views in an area designated as an Area of High Scenic Amenity in the Galway County Development Plan (An Bord Pleanála Ref. No. PL 07.096108, 25 Sept. 1995). This was one of the first recorded instances of a planning authority making a decision on a fencing scheme, which is normally treated as exempted development under the Planning Acts. The result of this decision is that the National Park staff find it difficult to prevent sheep straying on National Park lands, at least in the short term.

Domestic livestock are also allowed to stray into Killarney National Park. In Glenveagh National Park, an area of about 2,000 acres is set aside for sheep grazing, and there is a sheep fence inside the deer fence. The OPW won a court case over grazing rights when sheep were deliberately put through the sheep fence (this is not uncommon, and also occurs on State forestry land). In Wicklow National Park, it is accepted that there will not be a total exclusion of sheep, and there are differing views on the use of deer and sheep as grazers. In Killarney, there are grazing trials with Kerry cattle.

WORLD CONSERVATION UNION CLASSIFICATION OF PROTECTED AREAS BY MANAGEMENT CATEGORY

Category 1 — Strict Nature Reserve/Wilderness Area (e.g. in northern Scandinavia)

Category 2 — National Park, managed for ecosystem protection and recreation (e.g. all National Parks in Ireland)

Category 3 — Natural Monument, managed for conservation of specific natural features

Category 4 — Habitat/Species Management Area, protected area managed mainly for conservation through management intervention (e.g. Nature Reserves in Ireland)

Category 5 — Protected Landscape, managed for landscape protection, (e.g. English National Parks)

Category 6 — Managed Resource Protected Area, managed for sustainable use of natural ecosystems (e.g. Biosphere Reserves)

Source: IUCN, 1994. *Parks for Life: Action for Protected Areas in Europe*. IUCN, Geneva.

Management agreements Management agreements may arise in the future, with large landowners who are sympathetic to conservation. In other cases, the National Parks and Wildlife Service prefers to buy land and lease it back to farmers for grazing. Management plans exist for Killarney and Glenveagh National Parks, but only one has been published so far (OPW, 1990). A draft management plan has been proposed for the An Taisce property leased to Glenveagh National Park. Management Plans are in preparation for Wicklow and Burren National Parks.

Physical planning policy in National Parks

All development in National Parks was exempt from planning controls until the introduction of new Planning Regulations in 1994 (S.I. No 86 of 1994). In 1994, the Office of Public Works (OPW), then in charge of National Parks, applied to Wicklow County Council to retain a partially completed visitor centre in the Wicklow National Park. Construction had begun before a court decision that the OPW needed planning permission. The site was in a primary area of special control in the Wicklow Development Plan (see also Section 3.1). Wicklow Co. Council's policy in its County Development Plan precluded granting permission for this type of development. However, the Council gave permission without amending its Development Plan. In 1995, An Bord Pleanála refused permission, on appeal, for the visitor centre; one of the main reasons was

that the building would contravene the objectives of the Wicklow County Development Plan in relation to the designated areas of special control. This decision signalled a major change in planning policy for State developments in National Parks. Another partially completed visitor centre in the Burren National Park was ruled as an illegal development by the Supreme Court in 1994, prior to the new Planning Regulations. Subsequently, a planning application for the development was withdrawn in 1995, and a scaled-down development on the same site is currently the subject of a planning application by Clare Co. Council.

NATIONAL PARKS IN OTHER EUROPEAN COUNTRIES

The term, national park, conveys a different meaning in other European countries. In Britain, for example, national parks are, in effect, protected landscapes: most of the land is privately owned; landscapes are more strictly protected using planning legislation; farming and forestry are permitted; and strict nature conservation is confined to small areas. In order to clarify the definition of national park, so that comparisons can be made, the World Conservation Union has defined protected areas by the manner in which they are managed (see box above). Table 2.9 lists the National Park area in 31 European countries, the percentage area of the national territory occupied by National Parks and the entire protected areas of each country.

Table 2.9   Area covered by National Parks in Europe (IUCN Category II) by country

COUNTRY	TOTAL AREA (HA)	NATIONAL PARK AREA (HA)	% OF NATIONAL LAND AREA	TOTAL PROTECTED AREA (HA)	% NATIONAL LAND AREA
EU Countries					
Austria	8,385,500	76,000	0.91	2,081,300	24.82
Belgium	3,052,000	—	-	77,100	2.53
Denmark	4,307,500	—	0.95	1,387,100	32.20
Finland	33,703,000	393,500	1.17	2,728,100	8.09
France	54,396,500	2,613	0.48	5,358,600	9.85
Germany	35,684,000	13,100	0.04	9,192,800	25.76
Greece	13,198,500	60,400	0.46	221,000	1.67
Ireland*	6,889,500	47,287	0.68	65,382	0.95
Italy	30,124,500	471,900	1.57	2,274,600	7.55
Luxembourg	258,500	—	—	36,000	13.93
Netherlands	4,116,000	13,600	0.33	421,500	10.24
Portugal	9,239,000	21,100	0.23	582,500	6.31
Spain	50,488,000	132,500	0.26	42,450	8.41
Sweden	44,094,000	494,800	1.12	2,981,800	6.76
United Kingdom	24,488,000	—	—	4,951,300	20.22
Other European Countries					
Albania	2,875,000	9,600	0.33	34,000	1.18
Bulgaria	11,091,000	221,300	—	369,900	3.34
Croatia	5,653,800	46,300	1.99	385,300	6.82
Czech Republic	7,886,400	74,800	0.82	1,066,800	13.53
Estonia	4,510,000	176,900	3.92	439,800	9.75
Hungary	9,303,000	159,100	1.71	574,000	6.17
Iceland	10,282,000	180,100	1.75	915,600	8.90
Latvia	6,370,000	—	—	774,700	12.16
Lithuania	6,520,000	133,000	2.04	634,700	9.73
Norway	32,389,500	1,378,100	4.25	2,038,000	6.29
Poland	31,268,500	148,300	0.47	3,063,600	9.8
Romania	23,750,000	841,600	3.54	1,084,900	4.47
Slovakia	1,403,500	199,700	14.23	1,015,500	72.36
Slovenia	2,025,100	84,800	4.19	108,100	5.34
Switzerland	4,128,500			730,700	17.70
Yugoslavia	10,217,300	148,800	1.46	347,000	3.40

* IUCN figures for Ireland are slightly lower than the actual total protected area of the country, since small nature reserves have been excluded.
Source: IUCN, 1994. *Parks for Life: Action for Protected Areas in Europe.* IUCN, Geneva.

National Parks cover large areas of Eastern European countries such as Poland, Romania, Slovakia and Estonia. By contrast, England, Austria, Germany and France have larger areas of protected landscapes (Category V) than National Parks. Norway, Sweden and Finland have small populations relative to land area and larger areas designated as wilderness (Category I). However, statistics alone do not tell the whole story. The World Conservation Union concluded that only 10-20% of the c. 200 sites called National Parks satisfy the management objectives of Category II. Some parks in Eastern Europe are suffering from lack of resources due to changes in political regimes and quarrying and timber cutting are permitted. Air and water pollution have damaged some central European parks. Tourist facilities have damaged wildlife and spoiled natural landscapes and the pressure to develop such facilities is particularly strong in eastern Europe (IUCN, 1994).

EVALUATION
Site observation and consultation indicate that the National Park designation appears to have achieved its aims reasonably well, despite some

NATIONAL PARKS IN FRANCE

French National Parks were established under legislation passed in 1960. There are six Parks, five in mountainous areas and one in a maritime area. They are essentially protected landscapes (IUCN Category II) with special controls over economic activities, including farming and forestry, fishing and hunting. The Parks have a central zone (the 'zone parc'), where nature conservation is the principal activity, surrounded by a peripheral inhabited zone, the aim of which is to promote activities compatible with the central zone. The two zones are overseen by different Government departments. The park boundaries are a compromise between local administrations ('communes'), the state and naturalists. Land is owned by the communes and the Forest Service. The aims of French National Parks are to conserve nature and maintain the local community (in contrast to Irish National Parks, which do not include human habitation). No evaluation of French National Parks has been published.

problems with encroachment of livestock and several controversial visitor centre proposals. Entire areas of conservation interest can be effectively conserved (such as Killarney oak woods), which has not been achieved in practice by any other existing mechanism in Ireland.

Influence of National Parks on surrounding areas Irish National Parks are major tourist attractions, surrounded in all cases by areas where commercial activities take place (farming, forestry, tourism and leisure, fisheries, etc.) A zone of influence develops around National Parks which will have economic and social effects. For example, pressures may develop for tourist facilities on the park periphery. Local authorities may exercise stricter planning controls in the surrounding areas, especially for one-off housing. The interim Glenveagh National Park management plan identified a substantial 'buffer zone' surrounding the park. In Wicklow, some forestry grants have been refused by the Forest Service in areas surrounding the park because they conflict with nature conservation objectives in areas targeted for acquisition.

How might National Parks expand?
Expansion is a desirable option if nature conservation is the prime aim, and enlargement of National Parks would help to conserve a number of internationally important areas which may otherwise be degraded in the immediate future, including the blanket bog areas of North Mayo and Roundstone, and parts of the Burren. It has always been difficult

to practise conservation on private land in Ireland, since there is only a tiny minority of sympathetic private landowners. This may change in the future as public attitudes and incentives change, and allowance can be made for this.

The argument is often made that Ireland's landscapes are 'cultural' landscapes and need the intervention of man in order to protect them; therefore, setting aside large tracts of land for nature is at odds with Irish traditions, since Ireland's countryside is a living countryside, managed by traditional rural activities. However, most potential National Park land is in depopulated, marginal agricultural areas. If landowners are willing to sell land to the National Parks and Wildlife Service (NPWS), it would appear wise to acquire it. Where private land is managed in sympathy with nature, but the owners wish to remain, management agreements are an important option, especially in Wicklow, where State-owned land is separated by privately owned land.

There is no doubt that the public debate and controversy from 1991 onwards surrounding the building of visitor centres in Wicklow and the Burren has raised public awareness of the significance of National Parks, how they are managed and how they might expand. Because National Parks now assume greater importance as interest in outdoor pursuits and the environment grows, the management policy of National Parks may have to adapt to changing public expectations. Local community interests,

Upper Glen,
Glenveagh
National Park.

such as neighbouring landowners, might be given a greater role in the management of parks, which some are now asking for. The involvement of local people in a consultative capacity could help to resolve conflicts at an early stage, and could ultimately make the running of the park easier.

One option for future expansion of National Parks is to retain a 'core' area of State-owned land managed primarily for nature conservation, while a surrounding 'buffer zone' of privately owned land could be protected by planning controls, incentives and other measures. However, the core areas of Wicklow, Connemara and the Burren parks need to expand substantially to fulfil nature conservation objectives. The 'core and buffer zone' approach has been adopted in French National Parks (see box, page 40).

CONCLUSIONS

National Parks have been reasonably successful in meeting the objectives set for them, albeit over a very small total area. At present, all National Parks are State-owned. Visitor

pressure, at present, is relatively light. Staffing and resources are reasonably adequate *for the existing park area*. Further expansion will bring with it the need for additional staff.

The five Irish National Parks are small by European standards and the total area covered is only 0.68% of the national territory. Connemara, the Burren and Wicklow parks can be considered 'embryo parks'. A sixth park is planned for north Mayo. Expansion of National Parks would help to conserve a number of important ecosystems that otherwise are likely to be degraded in the immediate future.

Public expectations of the performance of National Parks are changing. More interaction between park authorities and the public is being demanded. National Parks will affect some economic activities in the surrounding areas. It is likely that their further expansion will partly depend on the support of stakeholders in surrounding areas, which will in turn depend on some input by local communities into policy making and management.

2.6

Refuge for Fauna

OBJECTIVE Protection of a named species of wild animal (vertebrate or invertebrate).

LEGAL BACKING Wildlife Act, 1976.

COVERAGE 7 sites; area not available.

RESPONSIBLE AUTHORITY National Parks and Wildlife Service, Dept. of Arts, Culture and the Gaeltacht.

POWERS UNDER DESIGNATION Ability to make compulsory management agreements on private land; ability to protect habitat requirements of the named species.

BACKGROUND

The Refuge for Fauna is a little-known and little-used designation for protection of one or more species of animals. It is, in effect, a compulsory management agreement, for which compensation is provided. Refuges are designated by Ministerial Order under the Wildlife Act.

DESIGNATED REFUGES FOR FAUNA

Seven Refuges for Fauna have been designated to date on cliffs and islands to protect breeding seabirds (see Table 2.10). All were made between 1988 and 1991. Protective measures include all potentially damaging activities that could take place in these inaccessible sites, such as cliff climbing and destruction of eggs and nests.

To date, no Refuges have been made which require action by, or land use constraints on landowners. The existing orders constrain the activities of the public generally, in habitats which are inaccessible and not subject to land use in the normal sense. None of the sites are under threat from development or land use change.

No compensation has been sought by land owners or users in respect of existing Refuges for Fauna. The sites designated to date are such that no compensation claims would be likely to arise.

Six new Refuges for Fauna are being processed to protect seabird breeding colonies, comprising one island group and five marine cliffs. None of

Rockabill, Co. Dublin, is a Refuge for Fauna, to protect a colony of breeding Roseate Terns, a species which is under pressure at its breeding and wintering sites internationally.

Oran O'Sullivan / IWC

Table 2.10 Designated Refuges for Fauna

NAME	HABITATS PROTECTED	SPECIES PROTECTED
Lady's Island, Co. Wexford	lagoon islands	Arctic, Common, Roseate, Sandwich and LittleTerns
Bull Rock, Co. Cork	rocky marine islands and contiguous seashore	Guillemot, Kittiwake, Puffin, Storm Petrel, and Razorbill
Cow Rock, Co. Cork	rocky marine island and contiguous seashore	Guillemot, Kittiwake, Puffin, Storm Petrel and Razorbill
Rockabill Island, Co. Dublin	marine island	Roseate Tern
Horn Head, Co. Donegal	marine cliff and contiguous 200 metre strip of sea	Common, Black-Headed and Herring Gulls, Cormorant, Chough, Fulmar, Guillemot, Kittiwake, Peregrine, Puffin, Raven, Razorbill, Rock Pipit, Shag and Twite
Old Head of Kinsale, Co. Cork	cliff top, marine cliff and 200 metre strip of sea	Chough, Fulmar, Guillemot, Kittiwake, Peregrine, Razorbill
Cliffs of Moher, Co. Clare	cliff top, marine cliff and 200 metre strip of sea	Chough, Fulmar, Guillemot, Kittiwake, Great Black-Backed and Herring Gulls, Peregrine, Puffin, Raven, Razorbill and Shag

the sites have any statutory protection at present. Seven sites are proposed as Refuges for Lesser Horseshoe Bats, a protected species.

MANAGEMENT IN REFUGES FOR FAUNA

Only two of the existing Refuges for Fauna are subject to management: Lady's Island and Rockabill, both of which have tern protection and research programmes. These programmes are run jointly by the National Parks and Wildlife Service and the Irish Wildbird Conservancy. No management is or can be carried out on the other refuges. Monitoring of seabird colonies is carried out under the Seabird Colony Register.

POTENTIAL APPLICATION OF REFUGE FOR FAUNA DESIGNATION

The designation has been extremely limited in its application because of the prevailing ethos within the National Parks and Wildlife Service which favours site acquisition rather than conservation management on private land. To date, no designation has proceeded where the owner of the land involved has objected.

CONCLUSIONS

The Refuge for Fauna designation is not widely used and has so far only been used in inaccessible areas with no development threats. Therefore, its effectiveness cannot be evaluated in a meaningful way. The legislation already allows for compensation. There appears to be no reason why compensation could not be used to facilitate landowners to carry out conservation management.

2.7

Wildfowl Sanctuary

OBJECTIVE Control of hunting, especially in wetland areas.
LEGAL BACKING Wildlife Act, 1976.
COVERAGE 68 sites; area not available.
RESPONSIBLE AUTHORITY National Parks and Wildlife Service, Dept. of Arts, Culture and the Gaeltacht.
POWERS UNDER DESIGNATION Control of hunting of listed species under Open Seasons Order.

BACKGROUND

Wildfowl Sanctuaries protect certain ducks, geese and waders from hunting, but their habitats cannot be protected unless by some other measure. Wildfowl sanctuaries have little significance in planning and development and are not normally recognised by local authorities.

LEGISLATION

Wildfowl Sanctuaries are designated, on State or private land, by Statutory Instrument under Section 24 of the 1976 Wildlife Act. In practice, landowners and local gun clubs are consulted before designation, and the boundaries can be a compromise, particularly on private land.

SCOPE OF WILDFOWL SANCTUARY NETWORK

There are 68 Wildfowl Sanctuaries. The area covered is not available. Table 2.11 shows the coverage of Sanctuaries for important areas for wildfowl.

Seventeen existing Special Protection Areas are at least partly covered by Wildfowl Sanctuaries, giving a small measure of protection from shooting. Forty-six sites are internationally important for waterfowl, and 21 of these have no protection from hunting.

Tacumshin Lake, Co. Wexford, a Wildfowl Sanctuary

Oran O'Sullivan / IWC

EVALUATION

Waterfowl learn quickly the areas safe from shooting, and this can affect their distribution. For example, bird use of Blanket Nook in Lough Swilly has increased since the designation of the Wildfowl Sanctuary there, and birds there are more easily monitored than in neighbouring sites subject to shooting (Sheppard, pc). In the Little Brosna callows, areas outside the sanctuary were seldom used by wildfowl during the open season (Mayes, pc). These examples indicate that Wildfowl Sanctuaries are effective in protecting waterfowl. Sanctuaries are patrolled by rangers, and prosecutions have been made against people found hunting within them. However, the few rangers lack sufficient equipment for the job, in comparison with fisheries protection staff who perform similar functions.

Table 2.11 Waterfowl sites covered by the Wildfowl Sanctuaries network

LEVEL OF IMPORTANCE	TOTAL NUMBER OF SITES	NUMBER OF WILDFOWL SANCTUARIES
International	46	28 (including 2 designations in each of 3 site complexes)
National	101	20
Regional/local	176	11 (including 2 designations for 1 site complex)
No count	—	8
Total	**323**	**67**

2.8

Ramsar Site

OBJECTIVE Conservation of wetlands, especially for waterfowl.
LEGAL BACKING None.
COVERAGE 47 sites covering 70,550 ha.
RESPONSIBLE AUTHORITY National Parks and Wildlife Service, Department of Arts, Culture and the Gaeltacht; Ramsar Secretariat.
POWERS UNDER DESIGNATION None. Ramsar Sites are protected only because they are also Nature Reserves or SPAs, and as such, protected under the Wildlife Act, 1976, or the Birds and Habitats Directives (see Sections 2.2 and 2.3).

BACKGROUND

The Ramsar Convention Throughout the world, natural wetlands are under pressure from development. The Convention on Wetlands of International Importance especially as Waterfowl Habitat — the Ramsar Convention — was adopted at Ramsar in Iran in 1971. For bird sites, a wetland qualifies for international importance if it regularly holds at least 20,000 waterfowl, or at least 1% of the population of a species. In terms of habitat, a wetland should be considered as internationally important if it is a particularly good example of a specific type of wetland characteristic of its region. The Convention notes the presence of rare, vulnerable, endemic or endangered plants or animals as a factor in determining international importance.

The Convention requires signatory governments to designate and conserve wetlands as Ramsar Sites but governments cannot be prosecuted for lack of implementation. However, a certain amount of moral pressure can be exerted through the Ramsar Secretariat. Sixty-five countries are now Contracting Parties under the Convention. The total number of internationally important wetlands designated as Ramsar Sites is 549, covering approximately 33,000,000 hectares throughout the world (CoE, 1992).

THE RAMSAR NETWORK IN IRELAND

Ireland ratified the Ramsar Convention in 1985 and has designated 47 Ramsar Sites up to 1997 (see Table 2.3 and Figure 2.5). Twenty-one sites are Nature Reserves, and two sites are owned by

Mongan Bog, Co. Offaly, (bottom left) adjoining the River Shannon. All Irish Ramsar Sites are already Nature Reserves.

Con O'Rourke

45

An Taisce and the Electricity Supply Board, respectively. All current Ramsar Sites are Special Protection Areas (SPAs).

Proposed Ramsar Sites A report prepared by the Joint Nature Conservation Committee and commissioned by the National Parks and Wildlife Service (NPWS) and the Department of the Environment in Northern Ireland proposed 49 bird sites for Ramsar designation in the Republic. Thirty-five of these were also proposed as SPAs (Way *et al.*, 1993). No new Ramsar Sites had been designated since 1990. In 1996, an additional 26 sites were designated.

Thus, the target of 49 sites has almost been achieved.

Protection of Ramsar Sites Ramsar Sites have no legal protection as such under Irish legislation. Their actual protection derives from other designations of the sites as SPAs or Nature Reserves. Thus, it would only be possible to assess the effectiveness of the Ramsar designation if applied to otherwise unprotected areas. The requirements of the Ramsar Convention for management and wardening of designated sites have not been met to date.

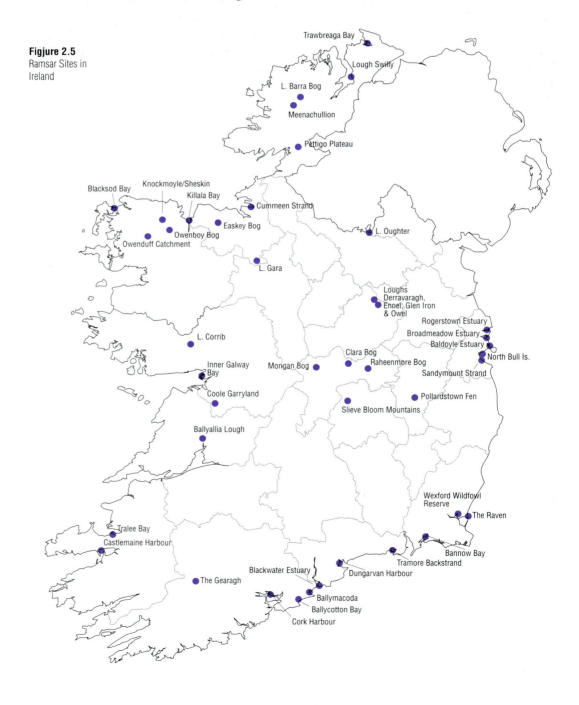

Figjure 2.5
Ramsar Sites in Ireland

2.9

Biogenetic Reserve

OBJECTIVE Conservation of representative examples of natural European heritage; scientific research and exchange of information.

LEGAL BACKING None.

COVERAGE 14 sites covering 6,587 hectares.

RESPONSIBLE AUTHORITY National Parks and Wildlife Service, Department of Arts, Culture and the Gaeltacht; Council of Europe.

POWERS UNDER DESIGNATION None. Biogenetic Reserves are protected only because they are also Nature Reserves, and as such, protected under the Wildlife Act, 1976.

BACKGROUND

Biogenetic reserves are designated by the Council of Europe, an international organisation which, in terms of influence, has been eclipsed by the European Union. The European Network of Biogenetic Reserves was first introduced in 1976. Member States of the CoE, including Ireland, agreed to identify and protect the natural habitats which are specially valuable for nature conservation in Europe.

BIOGENETIC RESERVES IN IRELAND

Currently, there are 14 Biogenetic Reserves covering 6,587 hectares, all of which are Statutory Nature Reserves, and only one of which is not State-owned (Mongan Bog, owned by An Taisce) (see Table 2.6, pages 30-31). All the Biogenetic Reserves already have other protective designations.

47

2.10

UNESCO Biosphere Reserve

OBJECTIVE To combine nature conservation with sustainable development; to create a worldwide network for research, environmental education and training.

LEGAL BACKING None.

COVERAGE two sites (Killarney Valley and North Bull Island).

RESPONSIBLE AUTHORITY Department of Education in Ireland; UNESCO.

POWERS UNDER DESIGNATION None. Biosphere Reserves are only protected by other measures.

BACKGROUND

So far, UNESCO has approved 324 Biosphere Reserves in 82 countries, representing the world's major ecosystems, of which 127 are in Europe. Biosphere Reserves do not have any legal standing (UNESCO has no powers to enforce them). However, it is assumed by UNESCO that countries will have already recognised and taken measures to protect qualifying sites. Biosphere Reserves are not supposed to be strict nature reserves *per se*. The main objective is to facilitate sustainable development, within certain zones, defined as 'core areas', for nature conservation. This idea has not been applied to the two existing Biosphere Reserves in Ireland to the same extent as in other countries, such as Germany.

SCOPE OF BIOSPHERE RESERVE DESIGNATION

According to UNESCO, Biosphere Reserves combine conservation, research and education within a single site and link these sites up to an international network, which made the biosphere concept different from more traditional means of protecting sites (such as reserves and parks) (IUCN, 1994). Biosphere reserves usually consist of a **core zone**, for strict protection of natural ecosystems, a **buffer zone**, which is more robust, to reduce the impact on

Bull Island, Dublin

David Hickie

A UNESCO BIOSPHERE RESERVE IN RHÖN, GERMANY

The Rhön region spans three German Länder — Thuringia, Hessen and Bavaria. Like many European landscapes, it is a cultural landscape which has evolved from man's interaction with the natural environment. Its distinctiveness arises from its special geological features, semi-natural forests, peatlands, species-rich meadows and pastures, and rare breeds. The variety of landscapes and their biodiversity depend on low input agriculture, which is fast disappearing. The Biosphere Reserve was made in 1991 over an area of 167,000 hectares (over 3 times the area of Ireland's five National Parks).

A number of projects have been initiated to promote sustainable development, including incentives for maintenance of traditional farming, conservation of traditional breeds, marketing of natural and cultural assets, and sustainable woodland management. Support comes from a new agri-environmental programme, EU Structural Funds and LEADER for marketing, training, farm tourism, technical advice and support for local crafts. EU Life funds support conservation activities. Money has been targeted on purchase and/or management agreements in the 'core' area of the Biosphere Reserve.

Source: Ute Böhnsack, personal communication

the core zone and a **transition zone** for sustainable development. The last principle — sustainable development — is heavily emphasised in the 1990s and was a far-sighted approach when introduced in the early 1970s. There is an implicit recognition of cultural identity, where man has a key role in maintaining biological diversity.

IRELAND'S BIOSPHERE RESERVES

In Ireland, the two Biosphere Reserves are Killarney National Park and North Bull Island. Killarney National Park has already been covered in Section 2.5.

North Bull Island, Dublin Bull Island was declared a UNESCO biosphere reserve in 1981. It is internationally important for waterfowl, the sand dunes, mudflats and salt marsh are botanically important, while the entire area is of earth science interest. Bull Island is also on Dublin's doorstep, which makes it of great educational value for natural history and conservation. The island has also been well researched by naturalists. All these qualities made the island unique in Irish terms and a candidate for world recognition. Bull Island has a peripheral, transition and core zone. Evaluation of the designation is complicated by the island's multiple designations, which are: Wildfowl Sanctuary, Special Amenity zoning in Dublin Corporation Development Plan (1980 and 1991), Special Protection Area, Ramsar Site, Nature Reserve, and Special Amenity Area Order (SAAO). The reserve is wardened, and siting of visitor facilities does prevent excessive incursion into the core zone. The northern end of the island is fenced to protect a colony of breeding Little Terns, while a barrier prevents access by motorists to the northern part of the beach.

It is significant that there are no local populations living *within* either of the two Biosphere Reserves. In international terms, both Irish sites resemble nature reserves more than Biosphere Reserves as envisaged by UNESCO.

Biosphere Reserves in Germany (see box) Germany has been involved in the UNESCO Biosphere Reserve programme since 1979. As of 1992, there were 12 Biosphere Reserves covering about 1,200,000 hectares (3.3% of the country), including the Bavarian Forest — the largest single forest ecosystem in Central Europe — and the Wadden Sea, an extensive area of foreshore and mudflats, important for wetland birds and fish.

Overall conclusions: Nature Designations

It should not be surprising that the nature designations which have best met the objectives set for them are Nature Reserves and National Parks, both applied almost exclusively to land owned by the conservation authority (currently, the National Parks and Wildlife Service). It has been difficult to conserve privately owned land, because:

- landowners respond to financial incentives. In many cases, State and EU grant and compensatory payment schemes, price supports, tax relief, and advisory services have directly or indirectly conflicted with environmental policies.
- the State has been reluctant to impose too many controls over private land. A strong rural constituency has consistently opposed such controls. For many, even the requirement for planning permission to build a house is seen as interference with the rights of private property.
- nature conservation is not a priority among the voting public. It is often not popular among rural communities because it is associated with restrictions. The folk memory of landlordism, with all that it implies, is still present in Irish culture, and the State is seen as another landlord, especially in the west of Ireland.
- planning and conservation legislation has always been interpreted in a liberal manner. Enforcement is not as thorough as in some neighbouring countries. This is a cultural phenomenon, which occurs in many areas of Irish life.
- practical knowledge of nature conservation is lacking among farmers, forestry workers, planners, engineers and others who are directly concerned with land management.
- resources for nature conservation are very modest and inadequate to meet growing public expectations and to fulfil EU legal requirements. Even resources for Nature Reserves are inadequate. Only in National Parks are staff and resources near to being adequate.

Since the introduction of the Natural Habitats Regulations 1997, which implement the Habitats Directive in Ireland, there is an expectation that extensive areas outside State ownership may receive some protection from damaging developments for the first time. There have also been some amendments to the Rural Environment Protection Scheme (REPS) applying to NHAs, SPAs and SACs, which aim to better integrate agricultural policy with nature conservation objectives (see Section 5.1). These are very recent policy developments which cannot be objectively assessed in this report. If the objectives for nature designations on private land are to be successfully achieved, a number of policy changes will have to be made, including:

- Common Agricultural Policy schemes, (e.g. livestock compensatory schemes, Ewe Premium scheme) will have to be better integrated with conservation objectives to curb overgrazing, water pollution and land reclamation;
- All relevant State agencies and local authorities would have to incorporate environmental objectives more fully into spending programmes and advisory services, and a directive from central Government would be necessary to achieve this aim;
- The National Parks and Wildlife Service needs extra qualified personnel to make management plans for SACs, Nature Reserves and National Parks, assess planning applications, supervise conservation works, and promote education and information programmes;

- Budgets for land acquisition and management agreements, especially for SACs, need to be increased substantially;
- Training in nature conservation is needed for all personnel involved with land or water management.

In political terms, these needs are demanding, particularly when they are seen as competing with other sectors. Reform of the status quo is slow, since it is not usually in the interests of the major lobby groups. The embargo on civil servant numbers severely restricts the National Parks and Wildlife Service from adequately carrying out its responsibilities. There is more reason for optimism since the passing of the Natural Habitats Regulations, 1997. The provision for compensation of landowners for proven loss of income in SACs has been crucial in gaining some acceptance of SACs by the

SPECIFIC RECOMMENDATIONS

NATURAL HERITAGE AREAS (INCLUDING SACs AND SPAs) AND NATURE RESERVES

- The Wildlife Act 1976 should be amended without delay to give protection to those NHAs not covered by the Natural Habitats Regulations 1997.

- The area covered by Nature Reserves needs to be doubled in the next ten years is order to protect those areas which cannot be conserved in National Parks or on private land.

- Staff and resource needs for nature designations in general are included in the General Recommendations (section 7.2).

NATIONAL PARKS

- Further expansion of all National Parks, where possible, should be encouraged and resources made available for this purpose.

- Draft legislation for National Parks should be passed without delay.

- The proposed National Park in North Mayo should be established.

- Consideration should be given for management agreements and leases with landowners where necessary, in order to expand park areas.

- Local people should be encouraged to participate in decision-making on management issues in and adjacent to the parks.

- An assessment of the effects of National Parks on the local economy of surrounding areas should be considered.

- Management plans should be completed for all National Parks.

- There should be less emphasis on resources devoted to infrastructure and more devoted to conservation.

OTHER NATURE DESIGNATIONS

- It is unnecessary to designate any further Biogenetic Reserves, since the objectives of the designation can be met by other measures.

strong rural lobby. Further amendments to the REPS have been made to curb overgrazing and habitat degradation which are improvements, at least on paper. Possible ways forward for nature designations are discussed in Section 6.

David Hickie

Lough Mask shoreline, Co. Mayo, with reedswamp and scrub woodland. Lough Mask is a proposed NHA and SPA.

Section 3
Amenity designations

3.1

Areas of Special Control in Development Plans

OBJECTIVE Protection of scenic landscapes and amenities at local authority level by means of planning controls.

LEGAL BACKING No direct statutory basis; indirect legal force through County Development Plans, provided for by the Local Government (Planning and Development) Act, 1963 and subsequent acts and Regulations.

COVERAGE n/a.

RESPONSIBLE AUTHORITY Local authorities.

POWERS UNDER DESIGNATION Control over all developments listed in Planning Acts, and outlined in Development Plan; no control over exempted developments (most agricultural activities).

BACKGROUND

'Area of Special Control' is used here as a generic term covering amenity zoning terms used by local authorities in their development plans, e.g. Area of High Amenity Value, Area of Special Scenic Importance, Special Policy Area, etc. In general, stricter planning controls apply within scenic landscapes, amenities and areas of ecological value. No official evaluation of these designations has been published.

Designation procedure Each local authority produces a draft Development Plan, which includes proposed or existing Areas of Special Control and their specific objectives. The Plan goes on public view for a specified period, during which Councillors and any member of the public may propose an amendment. The draft Plan is then presented to the Councillors, who can make additions or deletions according to a simple majority vote. The Plan is eventually passed and becomes Council policy. At any stage, Councillors can by majority vote amend Areas of Special Control by amending the Development Plan. Planning decisions are made by officials, not elected Councillors, and can be

Glendalough, Co. Wicklow — An Area of Special Control in the Wicklow County Development Plan. (Glendalough is also a National Park.)

Bord Fáilte

appealed by any member of the public to An Bord Pleanála (the planning appeals board). The Board's decision is usually final, unless a court decides that the Board acted in contravention of planning law.

Enforcement Areas of Special Control are enforced by Council officials who may grant or refuse planning permission for developments according to how they are considered to affect the scenic or amenity qualities of the area. For example, new rural housing can be regulated in this way, and many planning applications in rural Areas of Special Control involve new dwelling houses. Local authority officials may also consult with Government departments about developments outside their control, such as afforestation or mariculture projects. Local authorities may also consult with non-government groups for their views on certain exempted developments.

GOVERNMENT POLICY ON PLANNING AND DEVELOPMENT

Local authorities have the difficult task of balancing the needs of economic development with environmental protection. The above should be borne in mind when assessing local authorities' performance. In 1982, the Minister for Environment issued an important memorandum to local authorities: *Development Control: Advice and Guidelines* (DoE, 1982). The memorandum supported development, where possible, without an unduly restrictive approach to environmental protection. This policy was reinforced by a similar memorandum in 1992 (DoE, 1992).

Local authority zoning policies can be controversial, particularly when land prices are affected in suburban areas. In Co. Dublin in particular, a number of controversial re-zonings of agricultural land on the outskirts of the city were made by Councillors during the 1980s and 1990s which greatly affected land prices and development potential. Several Ministers have criticised re-zonings made by Councillors in contravention of the stated objectives of the development plan, particularly in Dublin and Kildare. In rural scenic areas, with which this report is mainly concerned, some controversial re-zoning has taken place, but it is generally accepted to be on a smaller scale.

EVALUATION

The performance of local authorities in upholding their designations is somewhat difficult to assess because some of the areas

---

EXAMPLE OF A LOCAL AUTHORITY POLICY FOR AN AREA OF SPECIAL CONTROL: CO. OFFALY

The objectives for protection of amenities and conservation in Co. Offaly are reasonably typical of local authority policy (see below):

— *to prohibit developments which would be visually obtrusive or which would detract from their intrinsic character and environmental quality (S. 2.5.3).*

— *to protect and preserve the County's primary areas of high amenity, namely the Slieve Bloom Mountains, Clonmacnoise, River Shannon, Grand Canal, Croghan Hill, Pallas Lake and Clara Bog and Eskers (S.2.5.2).*

Consideration is given to the following categories of development:

— *agriculture or forestry*
— *developments contiguous to existing settlements or clusters or to service a base*
— *tourism developments where adequate infrastructural services are provided*
— *housing for indigenous people providing that the location gives rise to minimal visual impact, that the design and construction is of a high standard and no other suitable site is available (S. 2.5.4).*

(Source: Offaly Co. Council Draft Development Plan, 1995)

Figure 3.1
Areas of Special Control
in Development Plans
(shaded). (Map compiled
by Cathrin Bickmaier)

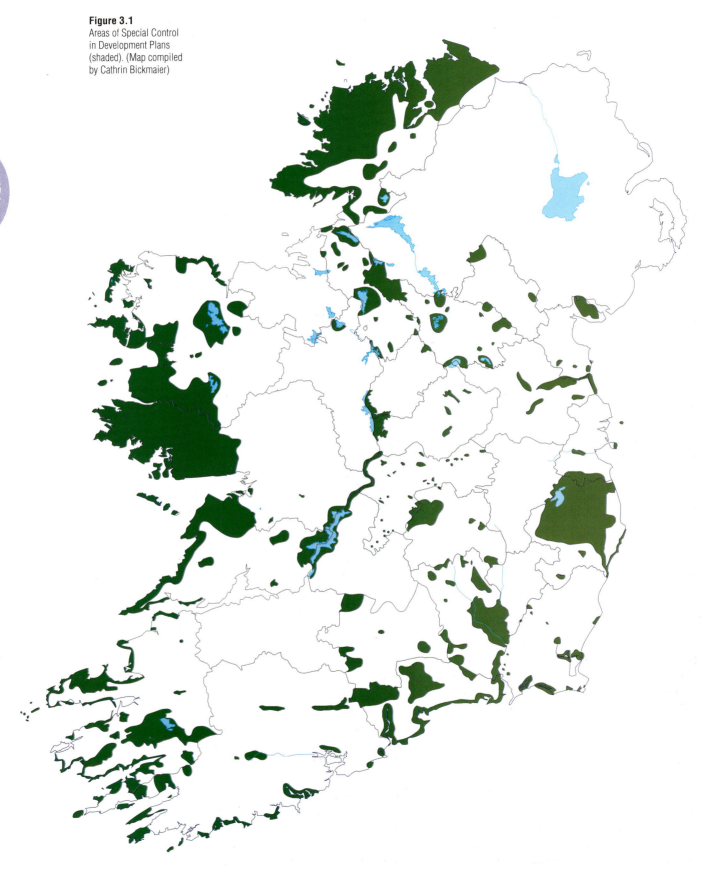

Calary Bog and the Great Sugar Loaf, Co. Wicklow, designated as an Area of Special Control in the Wicklow Co. Development Plan.

D. Hickie

designated may not, by their nature, be subject to development pressure (e.g. mountainous areas). Also, local authorities have seldom critically examined the effectiveness of their designations, and relevant data are difficult to access and compile.

Local authorities' performance is, in practice, highly variable. In general, most local authorities do not have the resources to enforce conditions of planning permission for all the developments granted permission. Performance also varies depending on the level of development pressure, the attitudes and training of higher officials, and the views of elected Councillors. There are many cases where planning officials try to uphold the objectives of development plans for high amenity areas, while elected Councillors and their constituents wish to facilitate development by amending or contravening the Plan. For example, a sand and gravel quarry proposed for Eskerbeg in Co. Roscommon, listed in the Roscommon County Development Plan as an ASI, was refused by the Council and subsequently by An Bord Pleanála in 1995 despite a majority of elected Councillors supporting the project. On the other hand, a few local authorities regularly contravene their own development plans in

relation to one-off housing in rural scenic areas (e.g. certain western counties).

The role of State bodies in the planning process State bodies, such as the NPWS, can have a considerable influence on local authority decisions. If the site of a proposed development has a national environmental designation, and it can be shown that such a site is threatened by the development, this could tip the balance towards refusal, either by a local authority or by An Bord Pleanála.

Role of An Bord Pleanála in the planning process An Bord Pleanála has set a number of important precedents relevant to Areas of Special Control. The Board is independent and is less influenced by *local* politics than are local authorities. However, Government policy will tend to influence some of its decisions. One example is the granting of permission for the Masonite plant on the banks of the River Shannon at Drumsna, Co. Leitrim in 1995. The developers stated that the proposed factory might be located elsewhere, with a consequent loss of jobs to a depressed region, if a quick decision could not be made. The Government and local politicians strongly supported the project. A forest plantation site was sold by the

Table 3. 1 Examples of refusals of developments by An Bord Pleanála in designated Areas of Special Control in County Development Plans

PROPOSED DEVELOPMENT	LOCATION	LOCAL AUTHORITY DECISION	AN BORD PLEANALA DECISION	AN BORD PLEANALA REFERENCE TO DESIGNATIONS IN REASONS FOR REFUSAL	DATE [AN BP REF. NO.]
Sand and gravel quarry	Castlesampson, Co. Roscommon	Refuse	Refuse	Recognition as a site of international scientific value and reference to County Development Plan objectives	17 Nov. 1995 [20.096448]
Wicklow National Park visitor centre	Luggala, Co. Wicklow	Grant	Refuse	Area of Outstanding Natural Beauty	10 Feb. 1995 [pl 27.094167]
Mineral water bottling plant	Manor Kilbride, Co. Wicklow	Refuse	Refuse	Landscape area of special control	19 Jan 1993 [27/5/89648]
100 houses and sewage treatment plant	Kilcoole, Co. Wicklow	Refuse	Refuse	Area of Scenic Importance	22 Jan. 1993 [PI 27/5/89410]
Leisure/hotel complex	Enniskerry, Co. Wicklow	Grant	Refuse	Area of Outstanding Natural Beauty. Dargle River listed as Salmonid Water in Development Plan.	24 Aug. 1994 [PI 27.093409]
Warehouse, sand, gravel and coal storage	Kilpeddar, Co. Wicklow	Refuse	Refuse	Area of Outstanding Natural Beauty	7 May 1992 [PI 27/5/87167]
29 residential chalets and roads	Brittas Bay, Co. Wicklow	Refuse	Refuse	Landscape area of special control	28 Feb. 1995 PI [27,094525]
3 houses	Bray, Co. Wicklow	Refuse	Refuse	Landscape area of special control	14 Dec. 1994 [PI 16.094195]
1 house	Mulranny, Co. Mayo	Grant	Refuse	Special Scenic Importance	
61 houses	Colonel's Wood, Westport	Refuse	Refuse	Area with objective to protect open space, provide for public open space and recreational purposes	7 March 1994 [PI 84.092377]
1 house	Rosturk, Mulranny, Co. Mayo	Grant	Refuse	Special Scenic Importance	24 May 1993 [PI 16. 090502]
Communications mast	Seefin mountain, Comeragh Mountains, Co. Waterford	Grant	Refuse	Area of High Amenity in County Development Plan	23 Mar. 1994 [PI 24.092118]
Hydro-electric power scheme	Lough Fadda/Lough Beg, near Sneem, Co. Kerry	Grant	Refuse	Special Amenity Area	12 Feb. 1991 [PI 8/5/82171]
1 house and 8 holiday chalets	Kilmore Wood, Co. Roscommon	Grant	Refuse	Area of High Amenity	26 Mar. 1992 [PI 20/5/86910]

Source: Taken from a sample of applications (1990 to 1995) referred to An Taisce, in its role as a prescribed body under the Planning Acts

Table 3.2   Planning policy decisions by An Bord Pleanála in relation to exempted development in areas of special control

DEVELOPMENT	LOCATION	EXISTING DESIGNATIONS	AN BORD PLEANALA DECISION [DATE]
Golf course	Maharees, Dingle peninsula, Co. Kerry	Area of Special Control; ASI	Not exempt [15 March 1993]
Golf course	Barna, Co. Galway	Area of Special Control	Not exempt [28 April 1992]
Golf course	Maharees, Dingle peninsula, Co. Kerry	Area of Special Control; ASI	Not exempt [1 June 1995]
Sand mining	Bishopsquarter, Ballyvaughan, Co. Clare		Not exempt [23 July 1993]
Farm roads	Iveragh peninsula, Co. Kerry	Area of Special Control	Not exempt [31 May 1989]
Commonage division, fencing and roads	Glenamaddoo, Mulrany, Co. Mayo	Area of Special Control	Fencing exempt Roads not exempt [13 August 1993]

State Forestry Board (Coillte Teo.). After the appeal, the Board's inspector recommended refusal on amenity and scenic grounds but the Board granted permission. One of the Board's reasons was that the site lay *outside* designated areas of special control in the Leitrim Co. Development Plan (An Bord Pleanála Ref. PL.12.096064, 20 Oct. 1995).

Table 3.1 lists a sample of refusals by the Board for certain developments in designated Areas of Special Control. In these cases, the Board upheld the objectives of the County Development Plan to protect the areas, and in all cases, these were listed as one of the principal reasons for refusing permission. Although An Bord Pleanála is not legally bound by development plans, in practice its decisions are heavily influenced by development plan objectives.

Areas of Special Control and exempted development Local authorities have no legal powers to control exempt development, but

GOLF COURSE DEVELOPMENT AT CLOGHEEN STRAND INTAKE, CLONAKILTY, CO. CORK

In the 1986 Cork County Development Plan, Clogheen Strand was designated as an Area of Special Control on ecological grounds, mainly because of its bird life. It is also a proposed Natural Heritage Area. The Development Plan stated that:

"It is the intention of the Council to protect these areas and views. Protection in this context means the strict control of any development which might prove injurious to the listed items..."

In 1995, the elected Councillors re-zoned the area as 'amenity land', against the advice of officials, in order that the Council could grant permission for the golf course without contravening its Development Plan. If the re-zoning had not been made, permission for the golf course might have been viewed as illegal under the Planning Acts, and could have been quashed by the courts. Permission was granted, under intense local political pressure, on 14 January 1995. An Bord Pleanála refused permission on appeal by environmental groups because the land was designated as an area of high amenity ecological habitat in the Development Plan and would therefore be "contrary to the proper planning and development of the area" (An Bord Pleanála, Pl 04.095259, 31 July 1995). Subsequently, drainage machinery attempted to reclaim part of the site for agriculture until a court injunction was taken. The above example illustrates the difficulties local authorities face in upholding their Development Plans.

CASE STUDY 2: LOUGH KEY AREA OF HIGH AMENITY VALUE

Roscommon County Development Plan lists the Lough Key area as the primary scenic amenity in Roscommon and has zoned it as an area of special control. There is a 'core area' (the lake and its immediate environs) and a wider 'buffer zone' (including the hills surrounding the lake). Planning applications referred to An Taisce by the Co. Council from 1989 to 1994 were examined. Only 40 planning applications were made within the zone during the period. Almost all applications for building within the core area were refused. Many of the applications granted were for houses in the surrounding buffer zone.

A large hotel and leisure complex at Rockingham in the core area was granted permission in 1992 by Roscommon Co. Council and An Bord Pleanála. Promised economic and employment benefits were clearly influential in the granting of permission. The permission did not allow for any disturbance to a Natural Heritage Area (native woodland) listed in the development plan. The development has not yet commenced as of May 1996. A marina at Knockvicar began without planning permission outside the 'core' area but within the buffer zone. The application for retention was granted, and granted again on appeal by An Bord Pleanála. It is significant that both the above developments were for tourism/leisure.

Bord Fáilte

Lough Key, the primary scenic amenity in Roscommon, zoned by Roscommon Co. Council as an Area of Special Control.

they have some influence through consultation with State agencies. Since 1989, the Forest Service has referred EU afforestation grant applications to local authorities if these are proposed for high amenity areas. The Service takes the views of local authority staff into account, although it is not bound to do so. Consultations with local authorities indicate that where refusal of grant aid is recommended, the Forest Service usually, but not always, complies. The consultation process is viewed as confidential by both parties.

An Bord Pleanála also made a number of decisions in recent years requiring certain exempted developments to be subject to normal conditions of planning permission, based on the 1977 Planning Regulations. Some examples are listed in Table 3.2.

The practical effect of the above decisions was to stall the above previously exempt developments until they could be examined under the normal planning process. The golf course in the Maharees was halted twice by council officials due to the need for planning permission; the development has not yet proceeded. The golf course at Barna was subsequently granted permission by Galway Co. Council and by An Bord Pleanála on appeal. Since 1994, golf courses require planning permission in the Planning Regulations, but it is likely that the previous Bord Pleanála decisions influenced the new regulations. The commonage division near Mulrany has yet to proceed.

The Cork County Development Plan contains some highly relevant statements that apply to all Irish local authorities:

"... listing in the development plan is not always sufficient by itself to protect areas from development pressures, and land of high scenic *amenity or ecological value but low agricultural value is particularly under threat."*

"The need for a means of acquiring and managing sensitive or ecologically important areas is becoming increasingly pressing."

"Over the years, there has been no diminution in the threats to these amenities and reliance solely on controls has not been as effective as circumstances would merit. Active involvement by the State, the Council and other interested parties will be necessary to ensure an adequate level of protection."

"The Council considers that legislative changes are required to address this matter" (Draft Cork Co. Development Plan, 1995) (see also Section 2.1).

It is significant that Cork Co. Council considered the purchase of areas of high environmental quality as one of the few solutions for their protection because of the difficulty of controlling development on privately owned land. It further indicated that central Government policy and practice in this area was inadequate and needed reform.

CONCLUSIONS

Areas of special control are key designations for landscape and amenity areas.

The degree of enforcement of planning controls varies from county to county, depending on the interest and commitment of officials and local politicians, the level of public participation, and the degree of development pressure. Local political considerations of wealth and employment creation play an important part in the decision-making process. Stated Government policy supports this position.

The making of the Development Plan and the planning process is now well developed and proceeds along democratic lines. The public could be included in the pre-draft stage of the Development Plan but would need some technical assistance to make a proper input. Development Plans could be improved by official guidance notes on key development issues, such as nature conservation.

The performance of local authorities in protecting Areas of Special Control is variable. An Bord Pleanála has made a number of key decisions in the past decade that underpin the significance of amenity and environmental objectives in Development Plans. It is possible for local authorities to protect landscapes and amenities under the present legislation, but local and national political pressure for development can make this difficult and can place great strains on decision-makers.

Lough Tay, Co. Wicklow, an Area of Special Control in the Wicklow Co. Development Plan

Bord Fáilte

Figure 3.2
The Liffey Valley,
one of the two areas
in Ireland subject to
a Special Amenity
Area Order. Map
shows development
pressures, inside and
outside the SAAO.
(Compiled by Naomi
O'Callaghan).

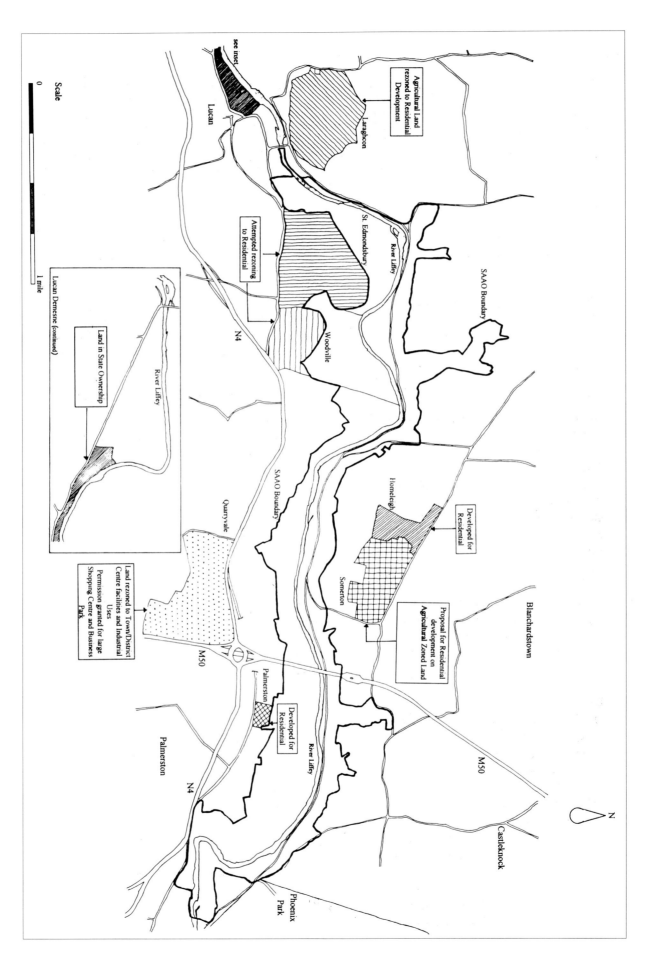

Special Amenity Area Order (SAAO)

3.2

OBJECTIVE To protect outstanding landscapes, nature, and amenities.
LEGAL BACKING Local Authorities (Planning and Development) Act, 1963.
COVERAGE Two sites (North Bull Island, Dublin; Liffey Valley, Co. Dublin).
RESPONSIBLE AUTHORITY Local authorities propose SAAO; Minister for Environment approves SAAO; local authorities enforce SAAO.
POWERS UNDER DESIGNATION Control over all developments listed in Planning Acts and outlined in Development Plan; control over some exempt development. Normal re-zoning is not permitted.

The Special Amenity Area Order allows planning authorities to strictly control development without the need for compensation and to control certain developments which are normally exempted. To date, only two SAAOs have been made — The Liffey Valley in Co. Dublin and North Bull Island, Dublin — although some other SAAOs have been proposed.

The main reason why so few SAAOs have been made is because of the strict control over development that they permit. The Order, although it must be approved by a local authority, must also be confirmed by the Minister for Environment, and successive Ministers have refused to confirm a number of Orders. This observation reinforces one of the central themes of this report, the respect for the rights and customs of property owners to maximise the commercial value of their property without undue hindrance from the State.

Designation procedure

a) The area proposed for designation should be of outstanding beauty, needing nature conservation or have special recreational value *in local terms*.

b) The designation is made by local councillors, not officials, and confirmed by the Minister for Environment, the Dáil and Seanad, and must be reviewed every five years.

c) An SAAO has a higher status than a County Development Plan because it may not be made, if objected to, unless a public local enquiry is held.

d) Some exempted developments can be controlled in an SAAO, and no compensation is payable for refusal of planning permission.

e) A nature conservation provision — the Conservation Order — can be made after an SAAO is confirmed (but not before). No orders have yet been made.

The area designated as an SAAO is shown in Figure 3.2. The area now designated was already zoned to protect high amenity areas in the Dublin County Development Plan. However, zoning is not considered as effective as an SAAO, as SAAOs cannot be re-zoned for development by a majority of local councillors, which has happened frequently in Co. Dublin over the last decade.

A number of applications were made to Dublin County Council to have some of the major estates in the Liffey Valley re-zoned to permit housing and other development. The SAAO study by Dublin Co. Council stated that

"in the absence of a coordinated management plan for the conservation and development of the valley, increasing development and consideration of development on a site-by-site basis may, if conceded, lead to the gradual erosion of the high amenity quality of the valley and prejudice the efforts of the Council to achieve its high amenity zoning objective".

(Dublin Co. Council, 1987).

Indeed, permission to develop on a site-by-site basis has resulted in the reduction of amenities and landscapes in many areas of Dublin and countrywide. The clear intention was to control development more strictly, using the SAAO. Even so, because of the intense pressure to develop land, certain areas were excluded in the final confirmation of the SAAO in 1990 by the Minister for Environment.

Dublin Co. Council published a management plan in 1992, but since then, the area has been divided between two new local authorities (South Dublin and Fingal Co. Councils). The Liffey Valley SAAO, because it was the first ever made, was deliberately conservative, in order to avoid possible legal challenges. A side effect of the designation is the view taken by some local politicians and developers that all Liffey valley lands outside the SAAO should be subject to development.

The Programme for Government in 1995 included an explicit commitment to proceed with a National Park in the Liffey Valley, as a result of lobbying by local interests wanting to protect the existing character of the landscape. The implication is that acquisition of land is the only way in which the landscape can be adequately protected. The reasons for the lack of faith in the Liffey Valley SAAO are (a) the limited area of the present designation to a narrow strip of land in the middle of the valley and (b) pressure for development without and within the designated area.

North Bull Island SAAO
The only other SAAO is for North Bull Island in Dublin, made in 1995. One of the main reasons given by Dublin Corporation for making the SAAO was to maintain the Island's Biosphere Reserve status (see Section 2.10). Most of the island is already owned by two public authorities and already has multiple designations: Nature Reserve, Special Protection Area, Ramsar Site, Wildfowl Sanctuary and UNESCO Biosphere Reserve. Thus, it is difficult to understand why a Special Amenity Area Order is necessary, apart from controlling developments which might be undertaken by the two golf clubs, which were stated by Dublin Corporation as unlikely to arise.

THE PROPOSED SAAO FOR HOWTH PENINSULA
The Minister for the Environment directed Fingal Co. Council to designate parts of the Howth peninsula in October 1996. A study has

Liffey Valley,
Co. Dublin

Undeveloped land in Howth, Co. Dublin. "Green Belt" areas such as this are subjected to intense development pressure, and could be designated as SAAOs.

David Hickie

been initiated in 1997 which will enable the Council to make a decision on designation, possibly in 1988.

CONCLUSIONS

Designating an SAAO on any privately owned land is likely to take a long time, in order to accommodate the many interests involved, especially property owners. Designating an SAAO in an area which is already reasonably well protected (i.e. Bull Island) would not appear to be the best use of local authorities' limited resources.

Designating an SAAO for land which is *not* already adequately protected, is under pressure from development and is of special amenity value, would appear to be a better means of protection than amenity zoning in a development plan. The SAAO would appear to be the best existing designation for protecting 'green belts' which are subjected to intense development pressure.

3.3

Tree Preservation Order (TPO)

OBJECTIVE Protection of trees, groups of trees and woods of amenity value.
LEGAL BACKING Local Government (Planning and Development) Act, 1963, Section 45, as amended by Section 14(10) of the 1976 Planning Act and Section 20(1) of the 1992 Act. Section 21 of the Local Government (Planning and Development) Act, 1990, as amended by Section 21 of the 1992 Act.
COVERAGE 178 designations.
RESPONSIBLE AUTHORITY Local authorities.
POWERS UNDER DESIGNATION Planning control over tree felling or any interference with designated trees.

Tree protected by a TPO, Carysfort, Blackrock, Co. Dublin.

David Hickie

BACKGROUND

The Tree Preservation Order (TPO) is one of two legal mechanisms for protecting trees (the other being the Felling Licence). Any trees which are the subject of a TPO cannot be felled unless the owner applies for planning permission to his local authority. The decision can be appealed in the normal way to An Bord Pleanála. Tree felling is also covered by the Forestry Act, 1946, which forbids felling of trees in rural areas without a felling licence issued by the Forest Service. Even if permission to fell trees covered by a TPO is granted by a local authority, the owner must also have a felling licence, unless the site is within a urban area or county borough.

Designation procedure

a) A TPO can be proposed by anyone. Making a TPO is the function of the County Manager, and not the elected councillors. The decision to make a TPO can be appealed to An Bord Pleanála.

b) When a TPO is made, the owner is legally required to apply for planning permission to fell the trees designated. The decision of a local authority can be appealed in the normal way to An Bord Pleanála.

c) A TPO can be made on a single tree, groups of trees or woodland. A TPO can only be made where the trees are considered to be of *special amenity value*, and cannot be made *solely* on the grounds of ecological value.

d) The local authority may be liable to compensate an owner if damage has been suffered or property values have been reduced.

e) No compensation is payable if

  – planning permission is refused for felling of trees or groups of trees, except woodlands, where the trees are of *special amenity value or special interest;*

  – where a condition for replanting is made in the interests of amenity;

  – in *woodlands*, where no more than 20% of the trees in a woodland are protected because of their *special amenity value or special interest;* or

CASE STUDY 1: ARDEE FOX COVERT, CO. LOUTH — 8 Ha. BROADLEAF WOOD

Ardee Fox Covert is a small broadleaf wood used as an amenity by local people. A proposal was made by Louth County Councillors for a TPO in their Development Plan in 1990. In October 1992, the wood was sold by Coillte Teo. to Ardee Golf Club, whose grounds adjoin the wood. A clause in the contract of sale stated that the character of the wood was to be maintained, apart from two small areas to be cleared for tees. In December 1993, five local councillors again proposed a TPO, but no action was taken. In September 1994, the golf club cleared approximately 100 mature trees without a felling licence. Following intervention by Louth Co. Council, the Gardaí and the Forest Service, the Council finally confirmed a TPO on the Fox Covert in June 1995. However, by this stage, 20% of the wood had been felled.

— in *woodlands*, where the local authority requires phased felling or extraction of trees over 20 years because of their *special amenity value or special interest.*

GOVERNMENT POLICY ON TPOS

Government policy for TPOs is set out in a number of circulars to local authorities. In each circular, the Minister has emphasised the importance of protecting trees and has reminded local authorities of the powers under the Planning Acts to make TPOs.

— Circular letter PD 1/86 of 21 January 1986 *Planning Authorities and the Protection of Trees* mentions the use of the development control process to preserve trees.

— Circular letter of 10 June 1987 *Planning Authorities and the Protection of Trees* urges local authorities to "make maximum use of their powers to preserve trees in the interests of amenity" and encourages the making of TPOs.

— Circular PD 1/94 of 7 March 1994 *Tree Preservation: Guidelines for Planning Authorities* sets out how the development plan can be used to protect trees, the TPO mechanism, the use of normal development control to influence development proposals in a way that "protects and celebrates existing mature trees and encourages new planting", and the enforcement powers available under the Planning Acts (DoE, 1994a).

CASE STUDY 2: TOMNAFINNOGUE WOOD, COOLATTIN, CO. WICKLOW — 64 Ha. MATURE OAK WOOD

In the late 1970s, Coolattin estate was sold to new owners, when the extent of woodlands was 800 ha. Felling then began, and Wicklow Co. Council made a TPO in 1978. By the early 1980s, most of the woods not covered by the TPO were felled. The owners subsequently applied to fell some woods covered by the TPO. In 1983, a felling licence was granted by the Forest Service for felling and re-planting of 160 ha., and Wicklow Co. Council granted permission to fell the trees covered by the TPO. In 1986, Wicklow Co. Council again granted permission for clear-felling and re-planting of 44.5 ha. covered by the TPO. In 1987, an application was made to fell the final 64 ha. of mature oak woodland, including 2440 mature oaks, in Tomnafinnogue Wood, which was refused by the Minister for Energy. However, in 1992, a new Minister granted a felling licence for 90% of the mature trees over a 10-year period. Wicklow Co. Council granted permission for the felling of trees covered by the TPO. Following a campaign to protect Tomnafinnogue, the Minister for Agriculture in 1994 granted £400,000 to Wicklow County Council to buy the wood, which is currently in protective State ownership. This was the only practical means of protection in the long term. The TPO was only effective in delaying the felling programme which was licenced by the Forest Service.

Table 3.3   Number of TPOs in Ireland in 1995

COUNTY	NO. OF TPOs IN 1993-1995	TREES, GROUPS OF TREES OR WOODLAND
Carlow	n/a	n/a
Cavan	None	n/a
Clare	1	Woodland
Cork	8	n/a
Donegal	3	n/a
Fingal	3	2 Groups; woodland
Dun L/Rathdown	8	n/a
South Dublin	n/a	n/a
Galway	None	n/a
Kerry	None	n/a
Kildare	4	n/a
Kilkenny	4	n/a
Laois	None	n/a
Leitrim	2	n/a
Limerick	2	2 Groups
Longford	None	n/a
Louth	4	Woodland; 3 Groups
Mayo	9	2 Woodland; Groups
Meath	6	Groups, woods and individual trees
Monaghan	1	n/a
Offaly	12	6 Groups
Roscommon	1	Group
Sligo	None	n/a
Tipperary NR	3	3 Groups
Tipperary SR	3	3 Groups
Waterford	24	n/a
Westmeath	17	n/a
Wexford	1	n/a
Wicklow	46	n/a
Cork Corp.	9	8 Groups; 1 individual
Dublin Corp.	2	Individual
Galway Corp.	None	n/a
Limerick Corp.	3	3 Groups
Waterford Corp.	2	n/a
GRAND TOTAL	**178**	

Note: A majority of local authorities responded to a questionnaire in 1995 which asked for an update on the number and type of TPOs. Data for counties which did not respond has been taken from the Department of Environment Annual Planning Statistics, 1993.

NUMBER AND DISTRIBUTION OF TPO DESIGNATIONS

Official statistics for 1993 list 151 TPOs presently in force. However, the numbers of TPOs per local authority listed by the DoE does not always concur with local authority statistics (see Table 3.3).

EVALUATION

On the basis of consultations with a number of local authorities, it appears that the number of TPOs is a function of the interest that the council has in protecting trees and, to a certain extent, the local interest in tree preservation. Meath Co. Council, for example, has recently considered making more TPOs. In Clare, TPOs are considered ineffective and none has been made recently. In Louth, a number of TPOs were proposed by Councillors since 1993 without success, until 1995. An alternative means of protecting trees is through the normal planning process, where the local authority imposes conditions in planning permissions. This method, however, cannot protect trees in situations of exempted development, such as agriculture or forestry. Two specific cases are shown below.

CONCLUSIONS

The TPO appears to be of limited practical use in protecting trees and woodlands in situations where they are under threat. Only 20% of a woodland, or phased felling over 20 years are non-compensatable reasons for refusal of planning permission to fell trees covered by a TPO, which is inadequate to protect the integrity of many amenity woodlands.

Many local authorities lack funds to buy threatened woodlands, and so official decisions on TPOs have been dominated by the risk of claims arising against the local authority by

David Hickie

affected landowners in the event that planning permission is refused. The lack of any TPOs in some counties indicates that tree preservation is not a priority of local government.

TPO trees adjoining development site, St. Helen's, Booterstown, Co. Dublin. Planning permission was given to fell a number of TPO trees in the former parkland.

Tomnafinnogue Wood, Coolattin, Co. Wicklow. TPOs are designated on mature trees in the shaded area.
(Reproduced by kind permission of the Ordnance Survey.)

Amenity designations: Overall conclusions

The scope and effectiveness of Areas of Special Control is to a certain degree dependent on local politics. National policy has an important influence as well, and local authorities have the difficult task of balancing both national development and environmental protection policies. Any legal measures to improve the effectiveness of designations might result in less democratic involvement. The Minister for Environment has the power to revoke re-zonings where this is not in the interests of proper planning and development, but no revocations have yet been made.

It is significant that the SAAO is the least used amenity designation. The SAAO could be effective in controlling development, especially in 'green belts'. Greatly increased public awareness might counter-balance the traditional political strength of property owners and developers which previously hindered the designation of SAAOs.

The Tree Preservation Order appears to be an ineffective designation. A new procedure for protecting trees could be to introduce a Tree Management Licence, which would be the sole means of controlling tree felling. This would broaden the 50-year-old felling licence procedure, but should have an added amenity/ environmental element. The Forest Service should be responsible for granting licences, in consultation with local authorities and other relevant state agencies. Special amenity value, special ecological value, and good forestry practice should be non-compensatable reasons for refusing a Tree Management Licence. Fines for violation of felling legislation should be increased to a maximum £20,000 per tree on indictment, plus the resulting land gain.

SPECIFIC RECOMMENDATIONS

Areas of Special Control in County Development Plans
- No legislative changes are necessary.

Special Amenity Area Orders (SAAO)
- The SAAO designation should be applied more widely to high amenity areas on the fringes of urban areas, especially in areas vulnerable to re-zoning. The SAAO should be regarded as an appropriate means of protecting 'green belts'.

- The designation of additional SAAOs has to be promoted politically, and guidelines should be issued to local authorities by the Minister for Environment.

Tree Preservation Orders (TPO)
- The Tree Preservation Order should be phased out and replaced by a Tree Management Licence, administered by the Forest Service. The new system should build on the existing felling licence legislation. It should be possible to protect any tree of amenity or ecological value. Fines for violation of new legislation should be set at a maximum of £20,000 per tree on indictment plus the land gain that results.

Section 4
Water designations

4.1   Salmonid Water

4.2   Sensitive Area for Urban Wastewater

4.3   Sensitive Area for Fisheries and Forestry

4.1

Salmonid Water

OBJECTIVE Maintenance of water quality for salmon and trout.
LEGAL BACKING Council Directive of 18 July 1978 on the quality of freshwaters needing protection or improvement in order to support fish life (78/659/EEC) ('Freshwater Fish Directive'); European Communities (Quality of Salmonid Waters) Regulations, 1988. S.I. No. 84 of 1988.
COVERAGE 22 rivers.
RESPONSIBLE AUTHORITY European Commission oversees Member State policies; Dept. of Environment makes designations; local authorities implement designations.
POWERS UNDER DESIGNATION Local authorities are empowered to maintain water quality standards.

BACKGROUND

Salmonid fish are effective water quality indicators because of their sensitivity to pollution. Most Irish rivers can still support salmonids, unlike many other European countries. However, the unpolluted fraction of Ireland's freshwater has decreased from 83% in 1971 to 65% in 1992. Eutrophication (enrichment of water from excess nutrients) has been steadily increasing. Agriculture is a major contributor to this situation, but poorly treated sewage and industry are also responsible. The rarest Irish salmonid, the Arctic Charr, may already be extinct in a number of Irish lakes because of pollution (e.g. Lough Conn, Co. Mayo).

SALMONID WATER DESIGNATION PROGRAMME

Ireland is legally required by the EU Freshwater Fish Directive to designate Salmonid Waters. Twenty-two rivers have been designated to date (Table 4.1 and Figure 4.1).

Table 4.1 Designated Salmonid Waters and responsible authorities

SALMONID WATER	EXTENT OF DESIGNATION	MAIN AUTHORITY
River Aherlow	Main channel	Tipperary South Riding
River Argideen	Main channel	Cork Co. Council
River Blackwater (Munster)	Main channel	Cork Co. Council
River Boyne	Main channel	Meath/Offaly Co. Councils
River Bride (Waterford)	Main channel	Cork/Waterford Co. Councils
River Brown Flesk	Main channel	Kerry Co. Council
River Corrib and Lough Corrib	Main channel and lake	Galway Co. Council
River Dargle	Main channel	Wicklow Co. Council
River Feale	Main channel	Kerry Co. Council
River Fergus	Main channel	Clare Co. Council
River Finn (Donegal)	Main channel	Donegal Co. Council
River Glashagh	Main channel	Donegal Co. Council
River Lee	Main channel from source to Cork City Waterworks at Lee Road	Cork Co. Council
River Leannan	Main channel	Donegal Co. Council
River Lurgy	Main channel	Donegal Co. Council
River Maggisburn	Main channel	Donegal Co. Council
River Maine	Main channel downstream of confluence with River Brown Flesk	Kerry Co. Council
River Moy and tributaries	Main channel	Mayo/Sligo Co. Councils
River Nore	Main channel	Tipperary North Riding, Laois and Kilkenny Co. Councils
River Slaney	Main channel	Wicklow, Carlow and Wexford Co. Councils
River Swilly	Main channel	Donegal Co. Council
River Vartry	Main channel	Wicklow Co. Council

Figure 4.1
Designated Salmonid Waters,
Sensitive Areas for Urban
Wastewater and areas likely to be
designated as Sensitive Areas for
Fisheries and Forestry.
(Source: Clabby et al. (1992);
DOE.)

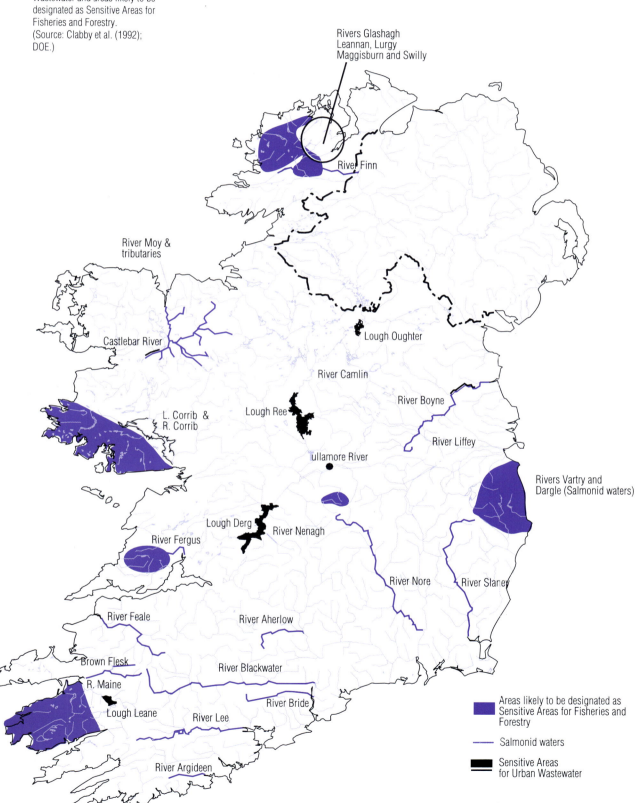

Rivers Glashagh
Leannan, Lurgy
Maggisburn and Swilly

River Finn

River Moy &
tributaries

Lough Oughter

Castlebar River

River Camlin

River Boyne

L. Corrib &
R. Corrib

Lough Ree

River Liffey

ullamore River

Rivers Vartry and
Dargle (Salmonid waters)

Lough Derg

River Nenagh

River Fergus

River Nore

River Slaney

River Feale

River Aherlow

Brown Flesk

River Blackwater

R. Maine

River Bride

Lough Leane

River Lee

River Argideen

■ Areas likely to be designated as
Sensitive Areas for Fisheries and
Forestry

— Salmonid waters

■ Sensitive Areas
for Urban Wastewater

ASSESSMENT OF WATER QUALITY IN SALMONID WATERS

The most up-to-date summary of results and analysis of data on Salmonid Waters are included in Water Quality in Ireland 1987-1990 (Clabby et al., 1992), which concludes that, on the basis of the results obtained by local authorities up to 1990, there was a satisfactory degree of compliance with the Salmonid Waters Regulations in the 22 listed rivers.

However, biological surveys undertaken by the ERU between 1987 and 1990 show that the situation in two-thirds of designated waters has not always been satisfactory. Water quality in 14 (two-thirds) designated Salmonid Waters, along certain stretches and at various times, was unsatisfactory, even though in general there was reasonable compliance with the Freshwater Fish Directive. The Boyne, Slaney and Nore are among the rivers showing signs of deterioration due to enrichment. Only 7 (one-third) of the designated rivers were recorded as unpolluted from 1986 to 1990 (see Table 4.2).

POLLUTION INCIDENTS IN SALMONID WATERS

Fish kills are an important early indicator of deterioration of water quality (Moriarty, 1994).

Silage effluent, animal slurries, poorly treated sewage, and industrial effluent are the most common causes in Ireland. Nine Salmonid Waters suffered fish kills from 1986 to 1993. The Feale had the greatest number of fish kills (15) in any one year, all of which came from a creamery discharging poorly treated effluent. The Blackwater and Nore also suffered from fish kills due to industrial or other pollution. Agriculture was responsible for at least 11 fish kills.

The viewpoint of the Fisheries Boards

The Fisheries Boards are the best placed official agencies to assess the effectiveness of Salmonid Waters designations. Their views are summarised below.

Advantages:

a) Continuous monitoring of water quality is mandatory, and this is invaluable when determining trends in water quality.

b) The Department of the Environment has not, to date, specified national water quality standards. If the criteria in the Freshwater Fish Directive were adopted for the entire country, a base for agreed water quality

The River Boyne, Co. Meath, designated as a Salmonid Water and Sensitive Area for Urban Wastewater.

Bord Fáilte

Table 4.2   Water quality of Designated Salmonid Waters from biological surveys conducted by the Environmental Research Unit from 1987-1990

1.	River Finn (Co. Donegal)	Mostly satisfactory, except at Stranorlar
2.	River Glashagh (Co. Donegal)	Satisfactory.
3.	River Swilly (Co. Donegal)	Satisfactory.
4.	River Maggisburn (Co. Donegal)	Continuing serious pollution from Milford to Lough Fern; deterioration since 1985.
5.	River Leannan (Co. Donegal)	Satisfactory .
6.	River Lurgy (Co. Donegal)	Mostly satisfactory, but lower reaches moderately polluted.
7.	River Boyne (Co. Meath)	Overall deterioration recorded since 1986.
8.	River Dargle (Co. Wicklow)	Satisfactory condition since 1986.
9.	River Vartry (Co. Wicklow)	Satisfactory.
10.	River Slaney (Cos. Wicklow, Carlow, Wexford)	Deterioration below Tullow and Bunclody since 1971, when no pollution was recorded.
11.	River Nore (Cos. Tipperary, Laois and Kilkenny)	Mostly satisfactory. Marked deterioration at Thomastown. Unsatisfactory in the Roscrea area.
12.	River Aherlow (Co. Tipperary South Riding)	Significant deterioration recorded in 1987 below Galbally.
13.	River Blackwater (Co. Cork)	Moderate pollution of some stretches. Seriously polluted below sugar factory in Mallow in winter.
14.	River Bride (Cos. Cork and Waterford)	Mostly satisfactory, but moderately polluted in the Bride Bridge area. Occasional pollution in other areas.
15.	River Lee (Co. Cork)	Below Carrigadrohid Reservoir was eutrophic. Otherwise satisfactory.
16.	River Argideen (Co. Cork)	Satisfactory, but signs of over-enrichment at several points.
17.	River Brown Flesk (Co. Kerry)	Inputs from polluted tributary.
18.	River Maine (Co. Kerry)	Moderately polluted below Castleisland, otherwise fair.
19.	River Feale (Co. Kerry)	Slightly polluted in upper reaches and moderately polluted below Listowel.
20.	River Fergus (Co. Clare)	Water quality fair at all points surveyed; no change since 1985.
21.	River Corrib and Lough Corrib (Co. Galway)	Satisfactory.
22. (a).	River Moy (Cos. Mayo and Sligo)	Mostly satisfactory. Moderately polluted below Foxford in 1989.
22. (b).	Moy tributaries (Cos. Mayo and Sligo)	Four tributaries suffering from some pollution; remaining tributaries satisfactory.

Source: Clabby, et al., (1992)

standards can be argued in relation to water pollution control, planning issues and EPA licence limits.

c) Designated waters receive a more favourable response for EU funding proposals.

d) The onus placed on local authorities to ensure that water quality is maintained to the required standard. A recognised standard is helpful when making submissions to local authorities or An Bord Pleanála.

Deficiencies:

a) Phosphorus, the major cause of enrichment of freshwaters — is not given priority. The limit of 0.2 mg/litre for phosphorus is inadequate, and a limit of 0.07 mg/litre for phosphorus would be more appropriate.

b) Only the main channels are designated, rather than the entire catchment (except for the Moy). Therefore, tributaries suffering from pollution cannot be included.

c) The designation is a 'stand alone' measure,

Salmon fishing on the River Moy, the only entire river catchment designated as a Salmonid Water.

Bord Fáilte

lacking integration with other wider measures, such as a river or catchment management plan.

d) Most, but not all, the rivers designated are relatively clean, requiring little expenditure for improvement but needing vigilance in maintaining water quality.

e) Many rivers have not been designated. Given that Ireland is one of the most important remaining areas for salmonids in Europe, it was felt that there should be a comprehensive list of designated waters.

f) Dissemination of the results of monitoring is inadequate.

g) Some other impacts, such as acidification and gravel removal from river beds, are not addressed.

CONCLUSIONS

The Salmonid Waters designation has been shown to be partially effective in increasing the importance of certain rivers as far as planning authorities are concerned. The main deficiencies are the limitation of designation to the main channel, rather than the river catchment, and the inability to address eutrophication. If these deficiencies were corrected, the standards in the designation could apply as national water quality standards. However, as with other designations, there are staff and money limitations in monitoring and enforcement.

4.2

Sensitive Area for Urban Wastewater

OBJECTIVE Protection of surface waters affected by eutrophication from municipal sewage.
LEGAL BACKING Council Directive of 21 May 1991 concerning urban wastewater treatment (91/271/EEC) ; Environmental Protection Agency Act 1992 (Urban Wastewater Treatment) Regulations, 1994. S.I. No. 419 of 1994.
COVERAGE 10 lakes and rivers.
RESPONSIBLE AUTHORITY European Commission oversees Member State policies; Dept. of Environment makes designations; local authorities implement designations.
POWERS UNDER DESIGNATION Local authorities are empowered to maintain water quality standards.

BACKGROUND

As towns and cities have increased in size, sewage treatment plants are often overloaded and dilapidated, giving rise to pollution. Coastal towns often discharge raw sewage. Microbes present in sewage can affect the amenity value of bathing waters and may contaminate shellfish, while excess nutrients, especially phosphorus and nitrogen, can lead to eutrophication.

Under the EU Urban Wastewater Directive, Ireland is required to designate Sensitive Areas. In 1990, the Government made a commitment to eliminate all pollution of inland waters from sewage discharges by the year 2000 (Ireland,

1990). Sewage treatment produces sludge which has to be disposed of. By the year 2000, it is expected that the current tonnage of sludge generated — 23,000 tonnes — will more than double (Colleran, 1994). Based on current estimates, about £1 billion will be needed to meet the provisions of the Urban Wastewater Directive.

DESIGNATION PROGRAMME

Designated waters are listed in Table 4.3 and shown in Figure 4.1. The basic requirement for designation of sensitive areas is that they be eutrophic, and that the eutrophication is caused primarily by sewage discharges.

Table 4.3 Sensitive Areas designated under the EU Urban Wastewater Directive (designated in 1994)	
DESIGNATED WATER BODY	**ASSOCIATED TOWNS (OVER 10,000 POPULATION EQUIVALENT)**
River Boyne	6.5 km section downstream of sewage treatment works at Blackcastle, Navan, Co. Meath
River Camlin	From sewage treatment works in Longford to entry into R. Shannon
Castlebar River	Downstream of sewage treatment works outfall at Knockthomas to entry into Lough Cullin, Co. Mayo
River Liffey	Downstream of Osbertstown sewage treatment works to Leixlip reservoir, Co. Kildare
Nenagh River	Downstream of sewage treatment works in Nenagh to entry into Lough Derg, Co. Tipperary
Tullamore River	0.5 km section downstream of sewage treatment works outfall in Tullamore, Co. Offaly
Lough Derg	Athlone, Nenagh and Tullamore
Lough Leane	Killarney, Co. Kerry
Lough Oughter	Cavan
Lough Ree	Longford

Source: Department of the Environment

Lough Ree, Cos. Westmeath, Longford and Roscommon. An EPA report recommended phosphorus removal in sewage treatment works of major towns and a code of good agricultural practice to reduce nutrient inputs. (Bowman, 1996).

All of the above rivers and lakes are eutrophic or showing signs of becoming eutrophic, according to the latest ERU water quality survey (Clabby et al., 1992). It is expected that when phosphorus reduction is installed in the above treatment works there will be a significant reduction in eutrophication.

The situation in Lough Derg and Lough Oughter is particularly serious. The ERU listed Lough Derg as "strongly eutrophic" and Lough Oughter as "highly eutrophic" in 1992, with both lakes showing no signs of improvement. Lough Leane is showing signs of improvement due to phosphorus reduction, while Lough Ree is listed as mesotrophic, but is considered vulnerable.

Existing phosphate reduction facilities in Irish sewage treatment plants are located in: Swinford, Co. Mayo; Bailieborough, Co. Cavan; Athlone, Castlepollard and Mullingar, Co. Westmeath; Rathkeale, Co. Limerick; Killarney, Co. Kerry; Castleblaney, Carrickmacross and Monaghan Town, Co. Tuam, Co. Galway.

CONCLUSIONS

It is too early to make an evaluation of the designation. The main advantage of designating waters under the Urban Wastewater Directive is the Government commitment to upgrade sewage plants by a target date. The designation does not address agricultural pollution, which will still affect many of the designated waters when pollution from sewage has been reduced.

Running costs of state-of-the-art treatment plants are high. As with other infrastructural development in Ireland, capital funds are readily available from the EU and Government, but not running costs. These have to be met by local authorities, which do not have unlimited funds for this purpose.

Finally, sewage treatment generates waste in the form of sludge, which has to be disposed of, probably to landfill. The quantities of sludge generated will increase significantly as more treatment plants come into operation.

Lough Derg, Cos. Tipperary, Clare, Galway and Limerick. The lake has been badly affected by sewage, industrial and agricultural pollution.

4.3

Sensitive Areas for Fisheries and Forestry
(proposed)

OBJECTIVE Protection of salmon and trout fisheries from the effects of commercial forestry operations.
LEGAL BACKING None.
COVERAGE Acid sensitive areas likely to be designated include: Wicklow uplands, parts of Donegal uplands, south Kerry, Connemara/south Mayo and north Cork.
RESPONSIBLE AUTHORITY Regional Fisheries Boards working under the authority of the Department of the Marine, Forest Service of the Department of Agriculture, Food and Forestry.
POWERS UNDER DESIGNATION No legal powers. EU afforestation grants are conditional on compliance with a code of environmental practice.

79

BACKGROUND

The dramatic expansion of industrial forestry in Ireland has damaged certain aquatic ecosystems through drainage, fertilisation and acidification. In the early 1990s, a number of State bodies decided to designate sensitive areas to minimise the environmental impacts of forestry. The targeted areas have yet to be designated officially, although the necessary information to back up designation is now available. The areas likely to be designated are the Wicklow uplands, west Galway and Mayo, parts of north-west Donegal, south Kerry and north Cork (see Figure 4.1).

DESIGNATION PROCEDURE

The following criteria apply to the designation of sensitive areas:

1. The aquatic zone must be part of a recognised salmonid fishery and be a spawning, nursery or angling area.

2. The geology must be base-poor (i.e. unable to counteract acidity).

3. In water samples taken between 1st February and 31st May — pH readings must be 5.5 or less, or water hardness must be less than 12 mg calcium carbonate per litre, or water alkalinity must be less than 10 mg calcium carbonate per litre.

HOW DESIGNATION WILL BE IMPLEMENTED

Although the designation is not yet officially made, it has existed *de facto* since 1993. The Forest Service, the regulatory authority for forestry, has published environmental guidelines in order to minimise physical and chemical effects on water quality (Forest Service, 1993). In reality, the guidelines are a code of practice, as afforestation grants are only paid if forestry companies adhere to the conditions. Since most afforestation proceeds only with grant aid, this has been a reasonably effective means of control. The guidelines include consultation with Fisheries Boards and measures to reduce the impact of ploughing and drainage, fertilisation, use of chemicals, thinning and harvesting.

EVALUATION

Since the early 1990s, field observation indicates that, in general, waterways are better respected since the environmental guidelines were introduced for sensitive areas. However, the guidelines are modest and do not address the cumulative impact of plantations in a water

Derryclare Lough,
Connemara, Co. Galway

David Hickie

catchment. The guidelines were a compromise between the demands of fisheries interests on the one hand and forestry interests on the other. Forestry interests are defensive about the link between forestry and acidification and have been reluctant to admit that it exists. There is a possibility that forestry companies could be liable for damages to fisheries.

CONCLUSIONS

Even though Sensitive Areas have yet to be officially designated, they have been in operation de facto since 1993. The advantage of the Fisheries and Forestry guidelines is that they allow for consultation, in advance of and during site development, between fisheries and forestry workers on the ground. On the negative side, there is no limit to plantation cover in a sensitive river catchment.

Overall Conclusions:
Water Designations

The Salmonid Water and Urban Wastewater designations appear to have been made independently as 'stand alone' measures in order to comply with EU directives. The Sensitive Area for Fisheries and Forestry is a national designation made in response to mounting pressure from fisheries and conservation interests to protect fisheries from damaging forestry operations.

The water quality standards of the Salmonid Water designation could be applied to many more salmonid bearing rivers in Ireland, but this would require more monitoring, which would tax the already limited staff and resources of local authorities. A national water quality standard, based on the standards of Salmonid Waters and with some important improvements, could be introduced, but this too would need more resources to implement than local authorities currently possess.

THE ROLE OF THE REGULATORY AGENCIES

The Regional Fisheries Boards have consistently proved to be the most effective agencies in enforcing pollution control, through the implementation of the Fisheries Acts. Local authorities generally have not yet demonstrated a willingness to use their powers to the full under the Water Pollution Act. A number of local authorities have shown a reluctance to enforce conditions of planning permission for intensive agricultural enterprises, such as large piggeries, or to make bye-laws to control slurry spreading. Very few local authorities have the capacity to enforce their own planning conditions. A few local authorities try to control the proliferation of septic tanks in unsuitable areas arising from one-off housing, which also contributes to rural water pollution. It appears that local authorities are compromised by their dual role as development agencies and environmental managers.

It is possible for local authorities to improve the enforcement of water quality standards under the Water Pollution Act without extra resources, but with political will. If conditions of planning permission for potentially polluting developments are unable to be enforced, local authorities could strongly consider refusing such applications, at least until adequate resources are available for monitoring and enforcement. Developers could also be required to contribute to the cost of monitoring and enforcement. Bye-laws with appropriate enforcement could be made more widely and could be supported by a consultation and advisory service for property owners.

FUTURE EU POLICY ON WATER QUALITY — THE RIVER BASIN APPROACH

Designation of waters in Ireland is primarily a response to EU directives. The EU is currently reviewing its water policy. In 1993, it proposed a new directive — the Ecological Quality of Waters Directive (COM(93) 680 final), the aim of which was to protect aquatic habitats, and by doing so, increase their value for drinking water and amenity uses. This would involve repealing the Freshwater Fish Directive, among other directives. The introduction of the Ecological Quality of Water Directive is now in doubt, and the European Commission in 1996 proposed a further directive, the Water Resources Framework Directive (COM(96) 59 final).

The proposed Water Resources Framework Directive signals a more integrated and cohesive approach to water management, on a river basin basis. Potentially polluting developments and activities will have to be assessed on the basis of how they might affect the entire river basin, instead of being assessed without considering their relationship with others. At present, local authorities and An Bord Pleanála examine planning applications on a case by case basis. The only State agencies promoting the river basin approach are the Fisheries Boards. The eutrophication of Lough Derg, for example, is partly the result of a lack of co-ordination among the many local authorities involved in enforcing planning and water legislation in the Shannon catchment.

If the Framework Directive is passed, Ireland may be required to designate certain river basins. This will require co-ordination of local authorities, or might need authorities whose responsibilities would span county boundaries. If planning and water pollution measures were approached on a river basin basis, agriculture, forestry and nature conservation policies could be adapted without too much difficulty, as these are organised on a national basis.

SPECIFIC RECOMMENDATIONS

Salmonid Waters
- Designation of Salmonid Waters should be on a river catchment basis.

- More rivers of salmonid quality should be designated.

- The Regulations should include a phosphorus limit of less than 0.1 mg/litre in order to address eutrophication.

Sensitive Areas for Urban Wastewater
- No alterations to existing Regulations are recommended.

- Attention should be given to environmentally sound disposal of the increased quantities of sludge generated by new and upgraded sewage treatment plants.

Sensitive Areas for Fisheries and Forestry
- There should be an upper limit for forestry plantation cover in designated sensitive river catchments.

Section 5
Other designations

5.1   Designated Areas in the REPS

5.2   World Heritage Site

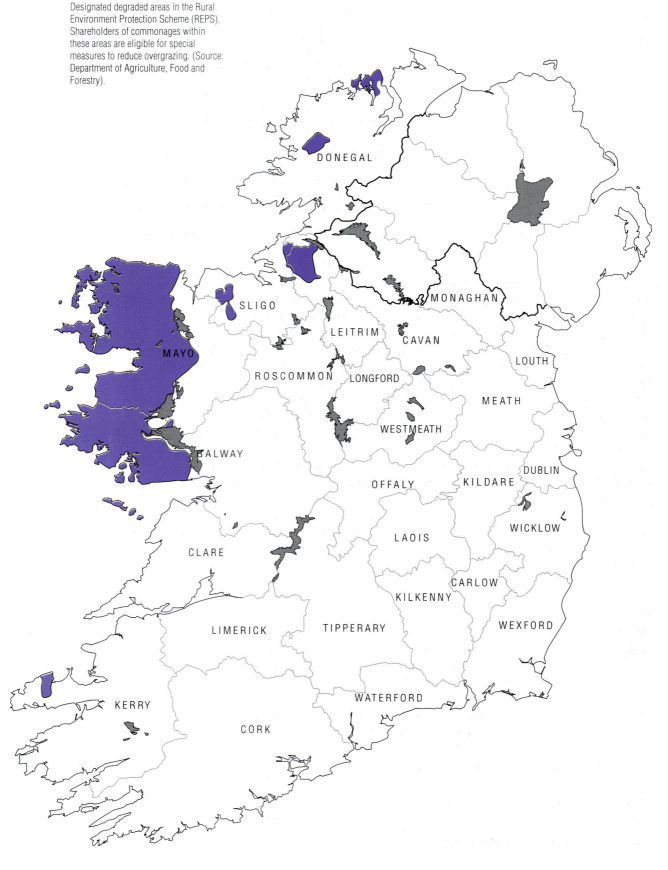

Figure 5.1
Designated degraded areas in the Rural
Environment Protection Scheme (REPS).
Shareholders of commonages within
these areas are eligible for special
measures to reduce overgrazing. (Source:
Department of Agriculture, Food and
Forestry).

5.1

Designated Areas in the Rural Environment Protection Scheme (REPS)

OBJECTIVE Conservation of natural and cultural features on farmland by voluntary grant schemes on a nation-wide basis and within certain designated areas.

LEGAL BACKING The Government is legally required to put in place an agri-environmental programme under EU Regulation 2078/92 of 30 June 1992 on agricultural production methods compatible with the requirements of the protection of the environment and the maintenance of the countryside (O.J L. 215/85). Funded by Irish exchequer and CAP Guarantee Fund.

COVERAGE Whole country; special measures in designated degraded areas, NHAs and Salmonid Waters.

RESPONSIBLE AUTHORITY Dept. of Agriculture, Food and Forestry (DAFF).

POWERS UNDER DESIGNATION Dept. of Agriculture, Food and Forestry makes payments to farmers, enforces payment conditions, appoints farm planners, and designates areas for special measures.

BACKGROUND

The Rural Environment Protection Scheme (REPS) represents a radical change in Irish agricultural policy, as it is the first nation-wide scheme to encourage farmers to protect the natural and cultural heritage. Any farmer may apply. Farmers who apply must prepare a plan for environmental protection (including pollution control) over 5 years. In return, the farmer is eligible for a maximum of £5,000 per year for 5 years for the basic scheme. In addition to the basic REPS, there are special incentives which apply to certain designated areas (see Table 5.1). The scheme operates from 1994 to 1999.

EVALUATION

In February 1996, over 11,000 farmers were participating in the REPS, costing £36 million and covering 381,600 ha. In March 1997, 23,279 farmers were participating, at a cost of over £82 million and covering 773,232 ha. These figures refer to the entire country and not specifically to designated areas. It would appear that the Department of Agriculture, Food and Forestry (DAFF) should achieve its target of 30% of all farmers participating in the REPS by the year 2,000. This target is set out in the Government's Sustainable Development Strategy, prepared by the Department of the Environment (DoE, 1997). No assessment of the effectiveness of the REPS has been carried out since it was introduced in 1994, since there is insufficient baseline data. It is therefore only possible to assess how the objectives of the REPS can be achieved and how the scheme has been administered so far.

Table 5.1	Special REPS measures which apply in designated areas	
SPECIAL REPS MEASURE	**OBJECTIVE**	**RELEVANCE TO ENVIRONMENTAL DESIGNATIONS**
Long term set aside	Conservation of river banks by set aside of land up to 30 metres from a river. Protection of bank from erosion and conservation of flora and fauna.	Applies only to designated Salmonid Waters (see Section 4.1) and some Bord Fáilte 'Branded Fisheries'.
"Degraded" Areas	Rejuvenation of areas suffering from overgrazing. 'Headage' payment for sheep removed from land.	Applies in designated areas identified by the Department of Agriculture (see Figure 5.1).
Natural Heritage Areas (NHAs)	Habitat conservation	Applies to landowners in NHAs (see Section 2.1)
Special Areas of Conservation (SACs)	Habitat conservation	Applies to landowners in SACs (see Section 2.3)

Source: Department of Agriculture, Food and Forestry

The Maumtrasna Mountains, Co. Galway, designated as a degraded area in the REPS.

David Hickie

Farm plans An environmental plan must be drawn up by an approved planner, who can be a private consultant or Teagasc staff. Many farmers, farm advisors and administrators are unfamiliar with nature conservation. The Department of Agriculture, Food and Forestry has approved planners with no previous experience of conservation management. Although such unqualified people can sub-contract ecologists to assist in the preparation of the farm plan, in practice this is uncommon. Department of Agriculture inspectors check plans and submit them to Head Office for final approval, which does not employ qualified ecologists. An unspecified number of plans have been approved which did not address wildlife habitat conservation. In March 1996, the Department of Agriculture, Food and Forestry refused to approve a number of deficient plans.

Monitoring and evaluation There is no legal requirement for evaluation under EU regulations. The Department of Agriculture has not put in place a system for environmental monitoring and overall evaluation. This is being considered, following pressure from conservationists and the European Commission. Currently, the only compliance measure is a spot check from Farm Development Service inspectors, where one in ten farms might be

The REPS is designed to encourage low intensity farming and conservation of wildlife habitats in designated areas and countrywide.

assessed. Because of the absence of monitoring, even at the end of the first 5 years of the REPS it may not be possible to assess its effect on habitats or water quality.

REPS in designated "Degraded Areas" (see Figure 5.1). Farmers in areas of commonage suffering from overgrazing can avail of a package of incentives to reduce stocking rates to sustainable levels in order to aid recovery of natural vegetation. Many of the affected areas also coincide with Natural Heritage Areas (NHAs) and Special Areas of Conservation (SACs) (see Figures 2.1 and 2.3). Until 1996, the incentives were insufficient to persuade farmers to enter the scheme, since there were better incentives under the competing Ewe Premium scheme. In 1996, the REPS incentives were made more competitive and include an incentive for groups of farmers to reduce stocking rates, and in some cases total destocking can be recommended. Only 216 farmers have participated as of March 1997, covering a total area of 7,606 ha., most of which are in Mayo.

REPS in Natural Heritage Areas (NHAs) Participating farmers in all the proposed NHAs receive a 20% 'top-up' (or premium) on the

David Hickie

basic annual payment if they adhere to guidelines drawn up by the National Parks and Wildlife Service in consultation with the Department of Agriculture, Food and Forestry. Observation of Figures 2.1, 2.3 and 5.1 shows that there is considerable overlap between Natural Heritage Areas, Special Areas of Conservation and Degraded Areas, most of which are peatlands or semi-natural grasslands. The REPS can therefore be seen as a potentially important instrument for nature conservation in designated natural areas. In February 1996, 1,079 farmers in NHAs were participating in the REPS (area coverage unavailable). By March 1997, there were 3,697 farmers participating, covering a farmed area of 115,641 ha., 50% of which is in Donegal, Mayo, Galway, Clare and Kerry. However, the Department of Agriculture, Food and Forestry figures do not specify the proportion of each NHA which is covered by REPS agreements. Therefore, the coverage of the REPS measure in an entire habitat type cannot be measured. The current management requirements for REPS in NHAs (introduced in late 1996) are an improvement on the previous scheme. Farmers in areas designated as SACs or candidate SACs are eligible for extra payments which are more generous than the NHA 'top up', which is limited to 40 ha. (100 acres) maximum. The SAC premium, introduced in March 1997, is extended to 120 ha. (300 acres). It is EU-funded and administered through the Department of Arts, Culture and the Gaeltacht.

REPS and long term set-aside in Salmonid Waters The long term set aside measure is restricted to designated Salmonid Waters (see Figure 4.1, Page 73), and other important salmonid rivers on the recommendation of the Regional Fisheries Boards. Participating farmers are eligible for payment of £450 per ha. set aside for at least 20 years. Each farmer is limited to 2.5 ha. set aside, and the strip of land is restricted to a maximum of 30 metres from the river bank.

Forty-one farmers participated in long term set aside of river banks (i.e. the 'riparian' zone), covering a total area of 57 ha. (December 1996 figures). The published data do not include the more relevant statistic of the length of the riparian zone of each river conserved. The long term set aside measure is potentially valuable for protecting river banks from erosion from livestock, thus enhancing the habitat for salmon and trout. The opinion of the Central Fisheries Board is that the measures are adequate to protect and enhance river banks and fish stocks. A problem with this measure is the restriction to a relatively small number of rivers.

CONCLUSIONS

In the first edition of this report, the Environmentally Sensitive Area (ESA) Scheme was examined. The Rural Environment Protection Scheme (REPS) has now replaced the ESA scheme, and the ESA designation has been excluded from examination in this edition.

Also in the first edition, the ESA scheme in Northern Ireland was contrasted with the REPS scheme in the Republic of Ireland. The ESA scheme is focused exclusively on designated areas, whereas the REPS is a countrywide scheme which has, *inter alia*, supplementary measures for some designated areas. It was concluded that the ESA scheme in Northern Ireland is more focused and better managed than the REPS in the Republic in terms of meeting environmental objectives.

Ministers and farm leaders have emphasised the role of the REPS as a social measure, and it was assumed that the REPS would automatically achieve its conservation objectives if a sufficient number of farmers participated. Examination of farm plans, consultations with a number of approved planners and observation on the ground lead to the conclusion that the environmental objectives of the REPS will not necessarily be achieved. The lack of adequate baseline information in REPS plans makes it difficult to assess the environmental effects of the scheme in the future. This further confirms the opinion that the REPS has been seen by the Government primarily as a farm income scheme with an environmental 'label'. In contrast, conservationists expected the REPS to be an environmental scheme with an added socio-economic benefit. However, there is no doubt that the REPS has increased environmental

87

awareness among farmers and this is likely to have beneficial results in the future.

The recent modifications to the REPS are a further attempt to encourage the participation of more farmers in Natural Heritage Areas (NHAs), Special Areas of Conservation (SACs) and Degraded Areas, while encouraging conservation by setting workable stocking rates for a variety of habitat types. Such areas include the Burren and the peatlands of Mayo and Galway, which had very low farmer participation rates in 1995/6. In March 1997, there were three times the number of participating farmers in NHAs compared with February 1996, accounting for with a farmed area of over 115,000 ha. This should be seen as a positive development.

The REPS could be a more powerful instrument for conservation if agricultural policies were properly integrated with environmental policies and if sufficient qualified people were employed to supervise, monitor and assess the scheme. The current REPS ends in 1999, and is expected to be followed by a similar scheme. An overall evaluation of the REPS, which has been indicated by the Department of Agriculture, would allow a new scheme to be more focused on achieving its environmental objectives.

Reference:
DoE (Department of the Environment), 1997. *National Sustainable Development Plan*, Dublin.

5.2

World Heritage Site

OBJECTIVE Protection of the world's natural and cultural marvels.
LEGAL BACKING None.
COVERAGE Boyne Valley Archaeological complex and Skellig Michael; 803 ha.
RESPONSIBLE AUTHORITY National Monuments and Historic Properties
Division, Dept. of Arts, Culture and the Gaeltacht (formerly the responsibility of the
Office of Public Works).
POWERS UNDER DESIGNATION None. Protection using National Monuments
Acts, and Local Government (Planning and Development) Acts.

BACKGROUND

The World Heritage Convention was adopted
by UNESCO in 1972 and came into force in
1976. World Heritage Sites cover both cultural
and natural features of world importance (e.g.
the Pyramids of Egypt, Stonehenge, the
Serengeti and the Grand Canyon). In Europe,
there are 120 cultural World Heritage Sites and
15 natural sites. Northern Ireland has one site
— the Giant's Causeway, in Co. Antrim,
owned by the National Trust. Scotland has one
site (St. Kilda Island). England and Wales have

eleven sites, all of cultural interest. All of the
UK sites are already protected by other
designations.

Ireland's responsibilities under the World
Heritage Convention to protect designated sites
include providing adequate staff and resources
for conservation, development of scientific and
technical studies and research to counteract
threats, provision of appropriate legal, scientific,
technical, administrative and financial measures
to identify, protect, conserve, present and

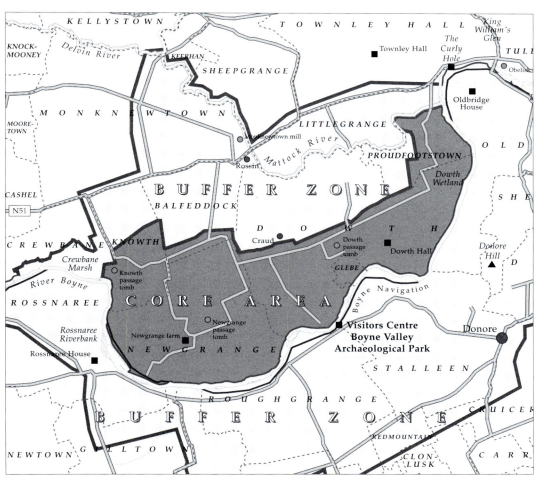

Figure 5.2
Map of the Boyne
Valley World
Heritage Site,
showing Core and
Buffer zones.
(Source:
Geography
Department,
Trinity College,
Dublin).

Figure 5.3
Map showing World Heritage Sites in Western Europe.
(Source: UNESCO).

◈ ◇ Cultural sites   ◯ Natural sites   ◈ Cultural and natural sites

rehabilitate sites. UNESCO can provide financial support, but also requires signatory countries to pay a contribution to the World Heritage Fund (UNESCO, 1972).

BOYNE VALLEY WORLD HERITAGE SITE

The only World Heritage Site in the Republic of Ireland is the Boyne Valley archaeological complex, which includes the world famous passage tombs of Knowth, Dowth and Newgrange, and many other antiquities (see Figure 5.2). The site includes a large proportion of privately owned land.

Over 20 years ago the National Monuments Advisory Council introduced the idea of an 'archaeological park' for the Boyne Valley. The site complex has been protected for at least this length of time by the Office of Public Works (OPW), using the National Monuments Acts. The local authority (Meath Co. Council) controlled development under the Planning Acts.

Policy of responsible authorities The management policy of the National Monuments and Historic Properties Division, (formerly in the OPW and now in the Dept. of Arts, Culture and the Gaeltacht), is:

"The managed landscape concept involves, essentially, the protection of the archaeological resource in its overall environmental setting while facilitating visitor access under conditions which are compatible with this primary objective of protection. This is achieved by the implementation of a local visitor-management regime, by the application of the National Monuments Acts and by the coordination of public and private land-use, while respecting the existing agricultural land-use pattern and social/economic activity" (Mitchell and Associates, 1994).

The policy of Meath Co. Council, covering the Boyne Valley, is:

1. "In Areas of High Natural Beauty and High Amenity, developments will only be permitted in exceptional circumstances...".

2. "Development which would erode the amenity value of the views and prospects listed ... shall be restricted".

3. "The sites and monuments listed in the OPW documents "Sites and Monuments Record (SMR) Co. Meath" shall be protected from development which would interfere with such sites or their setting and character. The Planning Authority will refer applications for development on or near such sites to the OPW..." (Meath County Development Plan, 1994).

EVALUATION

According to the World Conservation Union, the designation has been a powerful lever in preventing damage to listed sites in Europe. The unique passage tombs at Knowth, Dowth and Newgrange have been well protected. The World Heritage designation has only been applied since December 1993. Consultations with Meath Co. Council indicate that only about two or three planning applications each year for green field sites have been allowed since then. Potential applicants are informed in advance of these restrictions and so less applications are being made.

The most significant development since 1993 was the OPW visitor centre for the proposed Boyne Valley Archaeological Park. The centre was planned and construction began prior to the requirement for planning permission for such developments in May 1994. The centre is located outside the core area but within the buffer zone. One of its aims was to control the increasing number of visitors to the site. The location of the centre and its associated bridge and road improvements was opposed by some conservationists as being obtrusive in an area which remained relatively unspoilt. A number of alternative locations were rejected by the OPW and Meath Co. Council.

There is a large proportion of private land in the World Heritage Site. It remains to be seen if exempted development, such as agriculture, can be satisfactorily controlled in line with UNESCO requirements. A management plan for the Boyne Valley is currently being drawn up, with public consultation.

Overall Conclusions
Other Designations

In the first edition of this report, the Environmentally Sensitive Area (ESA) Scheme was examined. The Rural Environment Protection Scheme (REPS) has now replaced the ESA scheme, and the ESA designation has been excluded from examination in this edition.

Also in the first edition, the ESA scheme in Northern Ireland was contrasted with the REPS in the Republic of Ireland. The ESA scheme is focused exclusively on designated areas, whereas the REPS is a countrywide scheme which has, inter alia, supplementary measures for some designated areas. It was concluded that the ESA scheme in Northern Ireland is more focused and better managed than the REPS in the Republic in terms of meeting environmental objectives.

Ministers and farm leaders have emphasised the role of the REPS as a social measure, and it was assumed that the REPS would automatically achieve its conservation objectives if a sufficient number of farmers participated. Examination of farm plans, consultations with a number of approved planners and observation on the ground lead to the conclusion that the

environmental objectives of the REPS will not necessarily be achieved. The lack of adequate baseline information in REPS plans makes it difficult to assess the environmental effects of the scheme in the future. This further confirms the opinion that the REPS has been seen by the Government primarily as a farm income scheme with an environmental 'label'. In contrast, conservationists expected the REPS to be an environmental scheme with an added socio-economic benefit. However, there is no doubt that the REPS has increased environmental awareness among farmers and this is likely to have beneficial results in the future.

The recent modifications to the REPS are a further attempt to encourage the participation of more farmers in Natural Heritage Areas (NHAs), Special Areas of Conservation (SACs) and Degraded Areas, while encouraging conservation by setting workable stocking rates for a variety of habitat types. Such areas include the Burren and the peatlands of Mayo and Galway, which had very low farmer participation rates in 1995/6. In March 1997, there were three times the number of participating farmers in NHAs compared with February 1996, accounting for with a farmed area of over 115,000 ha. This should be seen as a positive development.

REPS could be a more powerful instrument for conservation if agricultural policies were properly integrated with environmental policies

Dowth, Co. Meath. one of the archaeological treasures within the World Heritage Site, Boyne Valley, Co. Meath.

and if sufficient qualified people were employed to supervise, monitor and assess the scheme. The current REPS ends in 1999, and is expected to be followed by a similar scheme. An overall evaluation of the REPS, which has been indicated by the Department of Agriculture, would allow a new scheme to be more focused on achieving its environmental objectives.

The World Heritage Site is an international designation with very demanding objectives, since such sites are considered unique in the world and need special protective measures. The only World Heritage Site in the Republic of Ireland — the Boyne Valley — is currently relatively well-protected and a management plan is being prepared. Very few other sites could qualify for World Heritage status in Ireland. Natural sites which might qualify include the Burren, Co. Clare.

SPECIFIC RECOMMENDATIONS

Areas designated in the Rural Environment Protection Scheme

- Environmental monitoring and assessment of the REPS needs to be put in place immediately. Currently, the quality of environmental information relating to REPS measures is either poor or non-existent. It is necessary to be able to measure the gains (or losses) to the natural environment as a consequence of the scheme.

- Qualified ecologists need to be more widely employed in drawing up and assessing farm plans.

- The REPS could be more focused on discrete 'problem' areas (e.g. the Burren as a unit is already subject to special REPS measures), or river catchments suffering from eutrophication.

- There could be greater use of incentives to encourage groups of farmers to participate in the REPS. (This has already been introduced for designated Degraded Areas.)

- The Ewe Premium Scheme, the Afforestation Scheme and other schemes need to be better integrated with the REPS if environmental objectives are to be achieved.

World Heritage Sites

The Burren as a unit should be examined with a view to including the region as a World Heritage Site, encompassing the existing National Park, and large areas of private land where ecologically sensitive economic activity would be encouraged and appropriately financed.

6

Analysis

A number of specific questions arise from the examination of environmental designations:

1. How do designations fit into overall environmental policy?
2. How do the different designations interact?
3. Is the number of designations an advantage or a hindrance for environmental policy?
4. What is the potential for streamlining designations?
5. How effective are designations compared with other policy measures?
6. Are there conflicts between environmental designations and other Government policies?
7. To what extent is the public involved in the designation process?

1. HOW DO DESIGNATIONS FIT INTO OVERALL ENVIRONMENTAL POLICY?

The main reason for designating areas or features is because they are considered to be of special interest or value. How important are the various designations in achieving Irish environmental policy objectives? This will depend to an extent on the scope of other measures which apply countrywide, as discussed below.

Designations are the central instrument in nature conservation policy. Nature designations cover about 7% of the national territory, while the remainder (93%) receives much less official attention. Nature conservation in the wider countryside has not been a priority and is poorly developed. The Wildlife Act, 1976 is still the only countrywide nature protection law, which has been almost impossible to enforce effectively, due to deficiencies in the Act, poor resources for the National Parks and Wildlife Service (NPWS) and other conflicting policies. The Rural Environment Protection Scheme (REPS) is the only countrywide agri-environmental incentive scheme, which is seen as a potentially important instrument for nature conservation. Although there have been some gradual improvements since 1996, the REPS still has a number of important deficiencies (see Section 5.1) which need to be resolved before the scheme can become effective. In conclusion, there appears to be an over-reliance on nature designations to achieve environmental objectives, often in response to EU directives, and insufficient attention given to nature conservation in the wider countryside.

Landscape protection is devolved to local authorities and is limited to areas designated in local development plans. There is no national overview of landscape protection such as in the United Kingdom.

Water protection policy is more highly developed than any of the foregoing. Improvements to sewage treatment plants, farmyards and other businesses are environmental priorities in terms of legislation and public spending. The Local Government (Water Pollution) Act, the Fisheries Acts, the Environmental Protection Agency Act and REPS are countrywide measures which assume greater significance for policy makers than designation of specific waters.

2. HOW DO THE DIFFERENT DESIGNATIONS INTERACT?

The overall impression is that each designation has been made in an *ad hoc* manner without sufficient attention given to related designations and other policies. Nature, landscape, water and agri-environmental designations tend to overlap with one another to a certain extent, yet they are often treated as 'stand alone' designations. Examples of the extent of the overlap are given below:

National Parks are all located in Areas of Special Control in the relevant County Development Plans because of their scenic beauty. Since 1994, planning permission is now needed for virtually all State developments in National Parks, and this is reinforced in Areas of Special Control.

Nature Reserves conserve wildlife but also often contribute to landscape quality. Many Natural Heritage Areas (NHAs) coincide with areas of scenic landscape, especially in the west, and many are listed in local authority development plans. Decisions made by planning authorities concerning NHAs are therefore highly significant.

Designated Areas in REPS include NHAs, Special Areas of Conservation (SACs) and Salmonid Waters. REPS has potential as an incentive for managing unprotected wildlife habitats. Currently, the indications are that the REPS is not acting as a disincentive to overgrazing or further intensification and reclamation in NHAs (e.g. in the Burren).

Some stretches of Salmonid Waters and Sensitive Areas for Urban Wastewater are also designated as NHAs or Special Protection Areas (SPAs) (e.g. Lough Corrib, Lough Derg). As yet, this overlap has not assumed importance. Sensitive Areas for Fisheries and Forestry coincide with undeveloped peatland or moorland areas with poor, acidic soils, usually peatlands. Often these areas are of scenic interest and zoned by local authorities as Areas of Special Control (e.g. Wicklow uplands). There is also some overlap with NHAs, especially in the non-forested areas of Wicklow, Galway and Kerry.

3. IS THE NUMBER OF DESIGNATIONS AN ADVANTAGE OR A HINDRANCE FOR ENVIRONMENTAL POLICY?

The large number of designations is not necessarily a disadvantage, if the measures under each designation are clearly understood and complementary, and if there is an overall coherence in the system. In terms of public perception, it can be a disadvantage if a succession of restrictive designations is applied to private land, and this can be seen as 'bureaucracy running wild'. The proliferation of designations is partly due to the legal imposition of EU Directives (i.e. SAC, SPA, Salmonid Water, Urban Wastewater). The EU

also requires designation for environmental health reasons (Shellfish Waters, Bathing Waters) and agriculture (Disadvantaged Areas).

4. WHAT IS THE POTENTIAL FOR STREAMLINING DESIGNATIONS?

Nature designations There are two basic grades of nature designations: National (NHAs) and EU (SPAs/SACs). Areas designated in either grade may then become National Parks or Nature Reserves. In practical terms, the other nature designations have only limited importance (i.e. Wildfowl Sanctuaries, Biogenetic Reserves, Refuges for Fauna). Biogenetic Reserves could be phased out, as the designation has been superseded by other designations. The Ramsar Convention could be useful as an extra lever for protection of some sites in the future.

Water designations An alternative to the Urban Wastewater and Salmonid Water designations could be a national water quality standard applied to *all* freshwaters, improving on the standards of the existing Directives. The EU is currently reviewing its water policies and a single new framework Directive on water quality has been proposed to replace all existing water quality directives. The outcome of this policy review is still uncertain. The Fisheries and Forestry designation is useful to identify sensitive water catchments in terms of their vulnerability to acidification.

Amenity designations Areas of Special Control and Special Amenity Areas Orders (SAAOs) can work effectively, and can be seen as grades of landscape protection. The SAAO could become an effective measure to protect 'green belts' which are vulnerable to politically-motivated re-zoning, while Areas of Special Control could continue to be used as a less restrictive planning measure. An alternative option would be to create a single landscape designation supported by national legislation (similar to the Area of Outstanding Beauty (AONB) designation in the UK), which would be applied by local authorities. A further option in some areas would be to apply the experimental Scenic Landscapes concept instead of formal designation (see page 97). The Tree Preservation Order (TPO) could be phased out

Table 6.1	Significant environmental designations		
NATURE	**AMENITY**	**WATER**	**OTHERS**
Natural Heritage Area	Area of Special Control in Development Plans	Sensitive Area for Fisheries and Forestry	Designated Areas in REPS
Special Protection Area/Special Area of Conservation	Special Amenity Area Order (SAAO)		World Heritage Site
Nature Reserve			
National Park			

and replaced by a national tree management licensing system (see page 70).

On above basis, the most significant environmental designations for the foreseeable future could be as outlined in Table 6.1.

5. HOW EFFECTIVE ARE DESIGNATIONS COMPARED WITH OTHER POLICY MEASURES?

Effectiveness of designations can be measured against the objectives set for them, but it also depends on public expectations, which are becoming more demanding. The essence of democracy is public participation, taking a range of interests in account, and imposing 'checks and balances' on elected politicians and their policies. The consultation process, in which a range of interests are taken into account, is being used more widely. It is inevitable that public participation will modify the way certain designations are made and how they operate (such as Areas of Special Control in Development Plans). Thus, certain designations may not meet the expectations of environmental organisations because the interests of landowners, the local economy and environmentalists have been balanced in order to reach a workable compromise.

Irish administrations have tended to rely on legislation to protect nature and amenities, and especially the designation of areas or features. Financial incentives, and educational and advisory schemes are becoming more acceptable as conservation measures, and the purely legislative approach is beginning to lose its appeal. Also, the concept of confining nature to small reserves, 'oases in the desert', has been out of favour with conservationists for many years.

There are cases where a designation may be ineffective because it is an unsuitable approach and not primarily because the legislation is weak or resources are inadequate (e.g. the TPO). On the other hand, this report has identified certain designations which could be improved by wider and/or improved implementation (e.g. Nature Reserves, SAAOs).

It is significant that in the United Kingdom, which has much stronger protection for designated natural sites in terms of legislation and enforcement, damage still occurs. Between 1987 and 1994, 800 cases of damage were recorded, 57 sites were partially lost and one site was completely lost (Bourn, 1994). England's protected landscape designations — National Parks and Areas of Outstanding Natural Beauty — are sometimes not as effective as public expectations demand. In Scotland, some conservationists are not in favour of National Parks because they could act as 'honeypots', focusing tourism development on areas that are not sufficiently robust to accept it.

EXISTING GOVERNMENT MEASURES TO HARMONISE ENVIRONMENT AND AGRICULTURE POLICIES

- No EU/State grant aid is available for afforestation in NHAs, SPAs and SACs, the effect of which has been to set aside about 50,000 hectares of blanket peatlands from commercial forestry.

- Capital grants to farmers for controlling farmyard pollution, supported by EU Structural Funds, have reduced the number of serious water pollution incidents (EPA, 1996).

- The REPS, introduced in 1994, is the first countrywide environmental incentive scheme for farmers.

However, conflicts between agriculture and environment policies include:

The Ewe Premium and Headage Payment schemes continue to encourage overstocking and unsustainable pressure on upland and coastal areas, especially commonage. Currently, although £230 million has been allocated to the REPS from 1994-1999, over £500 million will be spent on the Ewe Premium scheme during the same period.

6. ARE THERE CONFLICTS BETWEEN ENVIRONMENTAL DESIGNATIONS AND OTHER GOVERNMENT POLICIES?

This report has identified a number of such conflicts. For example, the effectiveness of nature designations on private land is undermined by agriculture, forestry, peat extraction, tourism and transport policies which are not sufficiently integrated with environmental policy. A similar policy conflict exists at EU level. If policies were harmonised, certain environmental designations (e.g. NHAs) would be more effective. Progress in this area is crucial to the effectiveness of nature and water designations (see box above).

7. TO WHAT EXTENT IS THE PUBLIC INVOLVED IN THE DESIGNATION PROCESS?

As public interest in environmental policy grows, so too does the demand for more consultation with officialdom. There is provision for extensive public involvement in amenity designations administered by local authorities. There is less scope for the public involvement with nature designations, although consultation with landowners and interest groups has improved in recent years. Since most current environmental designations involve some restrictions on development, local political opposition to designations often arises.

Antagonism to environmental policies will tend to reduce their effectiveness due to lack of cooperation by property owners and development interests. Alternatives to formal designation of landscapes and natural areas are currently being examined, notably the Scenic Landscapes Project undertaken by Bord Fáilte and An Taisce (Meldon and Skehan, 1996).

This is a landscape protection strategy which is dependent upon area-based landscape management which involves the local community. The strategy aims to anticipate and resolve conflicts between development and landscape protection. Empowering local people to take responsibility for the natural heritage, combined with offering attractive incentives for landowners, are vital factors for successful conservation.

7

General conclusions and recommendations

· ·

This report is concerned specifically with environmental designations. The conclusions and recommendations refer to wider environmental policy only where this is relevant to designations. Specific conclusions and recommendations are set out at the end of Sections 2, 3, 4 and 5. General conclusions and recommendations are presented below.

7.1 GENERAL CONCLUSIONS

1. **Lack of State evaluation:** There has been no thorough evaluation of the effectiveness of environmental designations by the Government departments responsible for their administration.

2. **Designations made in a random manner:** Environmental designations appear to be introduced in a random manner, without sufficient consideration of the effects that each designation may have on others. This reflects the sectoral basis of policy making in Ireland.

3. **Conflicting economic policies:** Sectoral economic policies (e.g. agricultural policy) tend to undermine the effectiveness of certain environmental designations. Designations will work more effectively if these sectoral policies are harmonised with environmental policies.

4. **Conservation on private land:** Private landowners are not sufficiently encouraged to conserve sites. This will continue to be the case until the package of incentives available to property owners automatically includes conservation.

5. **Sympathetic ownership — a key factor:** The full potential of nature designations can be best achieved if a suitable package

of incentives is made available to encourage conservation by sympathetic landowners.

6. **Limitations of indicative designations:** Designations without legal backing may be useful for identifying areas of special interest, but they are relatively ineffective in protecting the environment.

7. **Willingness to enforce designations:** The effectiveness of environmental designations is dependent on the willingness of the responsible authorities to monitor and enforce them.

8. **Lack of qualified staff and finance:** The effectiveness of designations is limited by the lack of sufficient suitably qualified staff and poor funding. Nature conservation, in particular, has always had to rely on a skeleton staff operating within a very inadequate budget.

9. **Designations and wider environmental policy:** Designations are only one component of environmental policy. There is a tendency for the State to over-rely on designations to achieve environmental objectives.

10. **Lack of local involvement in conservation:** Conservation has been seen as an interest of the State, and local people, including landowners, are not sufficiently involved in helping to protect natural sites and scenic landscapes.

7.2 GENERAL RECOMMENDATIONS

In order for environmental designations to be more effective, the following general recommendations are made:

1. **Economic policy**

   1.1 *Economic incentives*, such as capital grants, premiums, pricing, taxes and tax incentive schemes, need to be harmonised with environmental policies so that there is positive encouragement to conserve rather than degrade designated sites.

2. **Administration and management**

   2.1 Government departments and local authorities should undertake regular, transparent *assessments* of the effectiveness of designations for which they are responsible. This will require more resources devoted to *research* and *monitoring*.

   2.2 A significant number of additional *appropriately qualified* technical and research staff need to be appointed to the National Parks and Wildlife Service, the Department of Agriculture, Food and Forestry, and local authorities. These agencies are responsible for the majority of environmental designations and suffer from a serious shortage of ecologists and other suitably qualified technical staff.

   2.3 State *acquisition* of the most important natural sites should be accelerated.

   2.4 *Local authorities* need to be given a *directive* from Government in regard to the importance of protecting natural sites and amenity areas through the planning process, and in road, sewage and waste management programmes.

   2.5 *Local communities and landowners* need to be more closely involved with the protection and management of designated natural sites. This could be achieved through joint ownership and wardening of certain sites, and participation in decision-making through local structures.

   2.6 *Access to information* on natural sites and amenities is important to successful conservation. Officials, development interests, landowners and the general public need to have ready access to information concerning designations.

3. **Budgets**

   3.1 The National Parks and Wildlife Service (NPWS) budget for *land acquisition* and *management agreements* with landowners should be increased in order to meet the requirements of the EU Habitats Directive.

   3.2 Maximum use should be made of currently available EU funding to acquire priority habitats.

   3.3 Some EU finance should be made available to local community and voluntary organisations to acquire and manage habitats.

   3.4 The State should not have to provide all the extra funds needed for acquiring and/or managing natural areas. A *levy* on the *tourism* and *agri-food* industries, the key sectors which exploit Ireland's 'green image', should be investigated.

Appendix 1

RECOMMENDATIONS BY THE HERITAGE COUNCIL ON THE TRANSPOSITION INTO IRISH LAW OF COUNCIL DIRECTIVE 92/43/EEC OF 21 MAY 1992 ON THE CONSERVATION OF NATURAL HABITATS AND OF WILD FAUNA AND FLORA BY EUROPEAN COMMUNITIES (NATURAL HABITATS) REGULATION, 1997.

INTRODUCTION

The Council considers the European Communities (Natural Habitats) Regulation, 1997 which transposes Council Directive 92/43/EEC of 21 May, 1992 on the conservation of natural habitats and of wild fauna and flora into Irish law, as the most important legislation for nature conservation ever enacted in the State. Given the importance of the Natural Habitats Directive for nature conservation in Ireland, the Heritage Council makes the following recommendations at this early stage towards its effective implementation.

These recommendations are not in order of priority.

1. **That a financial commitment of sufficient scale be secured to enable the State to carry out effective monitoring to meet the habitat management obligations under the Directive.**
   The Council welcomes the landmark agreement reached between officials of the Department of Arts, Culture and the Gaeltacht and representatives of the farming community on a financial allocation to ensure that the implementation of the Habitats Directive is facilitated, and acknowledges the difficult negotiations which an agreement of this kind involved. The Council recognises that these measures are an important first step in laying the foundation for the implementation of the Habitats Directive, and welcomes the support of representatives of the farming community to achieve this end. However, equal effort should be applied to secure a financial allocation to enable the State to meet its obligations under the Directive in respect of biological monitoring, implementation of management plans, undertaking habitat restoration, etc.

2. **That sufficient resources should be provided to enable the National Parks and Wildlife Service engage in detailed discussion with all landowners, farmers, local authorities and other statutory bodies, to ensure that all parties have a clear understanding of the precise implications of SAC designation.**
   The designation of SACs can only be effective if there is a clear understanding of the implications of the designation for all users. Appropriate resources should be provided in order to enable the National Parks and Wildlife Service to engage in detailed discussion with all landowners, farmers, local authorities and other statutory bodies with the objective of ensuring that all activities within individual SAC sites are compatible with the objective of maintaining the favourable conservation status of the site.

3. **That each individual Special Area of Conservation should have its own detailed scientific programme so that the favourable conservation status of the site can be assessed.**

Article 11 of the Directive places an obligation on each Member State to undertake surveillance of the conservation status of priority habitats and species. Appropriate baseline data should be generated, and a detailed monitoring programme should be put in place for each individual Special Area of Conservation (SAC) in order to assess the conservation status of a site, and to ensure that the favourable conservation status of the site is maintained.

4. **That all individual SACs should have their own management plans, which incorporate mechanisms for assessing the effectiveness of the plan in achieving its objectives, and also provides for review of the objectives.**

All individual SACs should have their own management plans, drawn up on a site by site basis to ensure that the favourable conservation status of the site is maintained. This maintenance plan should be informed by the data gathering through the obligatory monitoring. Management plans should be reviewed and renewed on a regular basis, so plans should be drawn up on a five-year basis. Each management plan should incorporate the following:

- An assessment of the conservation status of the site, and the information on which this assessment was based. This should include baseline data on flora, fauna and habitats.
- Details of the programme in place to monitor the conservation status of the site.
- A clear statement of objectives.
- A detailed, scheduled work plan.
- Details of financial allocation to each specific task.
- A precise statement of what mechanisms are proposed to co-ordinate the activities of all players within the SAC.
- A schedule of publication of progress updates.
- A mechanism for reviewing the effectiveness of the management plan.

5. **That management prescriptions should be drawn up for all priority habitats, and that currently agreed REPS guidelines be revised to reflect the more stringent requirements of Special Areas of Conservation designation.**

The Council notes the intention to use the farming guidelines for blanket bogs, heaths, upland grassland and limestone pavement agreed by the Department of Agriculture, Food and Forestry, the Department of Arts, Culture and the Gaeltacht and the Irish Farmers Association for guiding management prescriptions for the SACs. These general guidelines were drawn up for the proposed statutory National Heritage Areas and are not to the standard required by SAC designation, since the latter are afforded strict legal protection, with a requirement to provide a detailed management plan. The guidelines should be tailored to the specific conditions of each individual SAC site. Adherence to the management prescriptions outlined in the farm plans should also be ensured.

6. **That the National Parks and Wildlife Service (NPWS) should have a direct involvement in drawing up SAC farm plans under REPS, and that additional resources should be provided to facilitate this role.**

The management prescriptions for farming within SACs should be consistent, irrespective of whether a farmer avails of the REPS or not. The Council accepts that, from an administrative and funding perspective, there are distinctions between those farmers who avail of the REPS and those who wish to remain outside the scheme. Nevertheless, all SAC farm plans should be overseen by the competent statutory authority for nature conservation, which, in this instance, is the NPWS. This would require considerable additional funding for the National Parks and Wildlife Service.

7. **That the National Parks and Wildlife Service should proceed with designation of all Special Areas of Conservation as a**

101

matter of urgency, but until all sites are designated, sites under threat of damage should be identified for the purpose of immediate designation.

While the regulations transposing the Habitats Directive into Irish law are now signed, strict protection is not afforded to Special Areas of Conservation until the landowners are notified of the designation. The Council is concerned that, given the limited resources of the National Parks and Wildlife Service, it may be some time before all sites of importance are afforded strict protection.

8. **That the criteria used for drawing the Special Area of Conservation boundaries of each priority habitat be published.**

The designation and delimitation of SACs is the key element in the implementation of the Habitats Directive, and the Council is aware that there are many potential problems associated with the process. As the identification and delimitation of all sites of community importance is based on strict scientific criteria, a point clarified by the Court of Justice of the European Communities in their judgement of 11 July

1996 (Lappel Bank case), these criteria should be published. The criteria for selecting sites eligible for identification as sites of community importance and designation as SACs are already published as Annex III of the Habitats Directive. The criteria employed by the National Parks and Wildlife Service for drawing the boundary of each priority habitat should be published to ensure the adequate assessment of the scientific justification for the drawing of each individual SAC boundary. This will greatly assist the work of the proposed advisory group in assessing the merits of any appeal.

9. **That the Advisory Group should contain sufficient expertise to assess appeals on a scientific basis.**

The Council welcomes the proposal by the Minister to establish an advisory group to consider appeals to SAC designation. As SACs are designated strictly on a scientific basis, the ability to assess appeals on a scientific basis must be the overriding criterion for selecting members to sit on this board.

The Heritage Council,
July, 1997

Acknowledgements

· ·

Grateful thanks are due to the following for their information, advice or assistance in the preparation of this report:

Richard Nairn, Natural Environment Consultants, Ashford, Co. Wicklow and Eleanor Mayes, independent environmental consultant, The Old Post Office, Ashford, Co. Wicklow, who were employed as consultants for the study which formed the basis for this publication. Their survey and research work on NHAs, Nature Reserves, SPAs, Wildfowl Sanctuaries, Refuges for Fauna and Biogenetic Reserves is summarised in this report.

John O'Sullivan, Valerie Bond, Naomi O'Callaghan, Margaret Sweeney, Frank Convery, Emer Colleran, Ken Mawhinney, John Feehan, David Meehan, Jack Durand, Helga Willer, Ute Böhnsack, J.V. Rice, Cathrin Bickmaier.

Managers and environmental officers in the Western, North-Western, Southern, South-Western, Northern, Shannon, Eastern and Regional Fisheries Boards. Staff at the Central Fisheries Board. Staff at the Department of the Marine and BIM.

Tony McCullough, Alan Craig and staff at the National Parks and Wildlife Service. Eugene Keane the National Monuments and Historic Properties Service of the Department of Arts, Culture and the Gaeltacht. Noel Lynch and Margaret Nealon at the Department of Arts, Culture and the Gaeltacht. Tony Roche, Photo Library, Office of Public Works.

The Environmental Protection Agency.

Diarmiud McAree in the Forest Service of the Department of Agriculture, Food and Forestry. Staff in the Environment Section of the Department of Agriculture, Food and Forestry.

Officials in the following local authorities: Meath, Louth, Fingal, South Dublin, Wicklow, Cork, Clare, Offaly, Sligo, Roscommon.

Paul Ryan and Anne Costello at the Department of Environment.

Mrs Rossler at the World Heritage Centre, UNESCO, Paris.

The Irish Peatland Conservation Council, the Royal Society for the Protection of Birds in Northern Ireland, and the Irish Wildbird Conservancy.

Katrina Bouchier, Environmental Publications.

103

References

AFF (An Foras Forbartha), 1981. *National Heritage Inventory: Areas of Scientific Interest in Ireland.* Dublin.

Bourn, J. 1994. *Protecting and managing sites of Special Scientific Interest in England.* Report by the Comptroller and Auditor-General. HMSO. London.

Bowman, J.J., 1996. *Lough Ree: An Investigation of Eutrophication and its causes.* Environmental Protection Agency, Wexford.

Cabot, D (Ed). 1985. *The State of the Environment: A report prepared for the Minister for the Environment.* An Foras Forbartha, Dublin.

Clabby, K.J., Lucey, J., McGarrigle, M.L., Bowman, J.J., Flanagan, P.J. and P.F. Toner. 1992. *Water Quality in Ireland 1987-1990.* Environmental Research Unit. St Martin's House, Waterloo Road, Dublin.

CoE (Council of Europe), 1992. Naturopa Newsletter No. 92-4. Council of Europe, PO Box 431 R6, F-67006, Strasbourg, France.

Colleran, E., 1994. Waste Management. Sweeney, G. ed. *Environmental Management, Development and Control,* Vol. 2. Built Environment Research Centre and Dublin Institute of Technology. Dublin.

Craig, A. 1984. National Parks and other Conservation Areas. In: Jeffrey, D.W. (Ed.) *Nature Conservation in Ireland: Progress and Problems.* Royal Irish Academy, Dublin.

DoE (Department of Environment), 1982. Development Control: Advice and Guidelines. Department of Environment Circular PD 9/82 of 26 October 1982.

DoE (Department of Environment), 1992. Development Control: Advice and Guidelines. Department of Environment Circular PD 2/92 of 17 January 1992.

DoE (Department of Environment), 1994. Tree Preservation: Guidelines for Planning Authorities. Department of Environment Circular PD 1/94 of 7 March 1994.

Dublin Co. Council, 1987. Liffey Valley Special Amenity Area Study. Lucan Bridge to Palmerstown. Planning Department, Dublin Co. Council, September 1987.

Erdmann, K. H, and Nauber, J. 1994. Der deutsche Beitrag zum UNESCO-Program "Der Mensch und die Biosphäre". *Deutsches Nationalkomitee für das UNESCO-Programm "Der Mensch und die Biosphäre (MAB)",* UNESCO, Paris.

Forest Service, 1993. Environmental Guidelines for Archaeology, Fisheries and Landscape. Series of three leaflets. Forest Service, Dept. of Agriculture, Food and Forestry, Dublin.

IPCC (Irish Peatland Conservation Council), 1996. *IPCC Conservation Plan 2000.* IPCC, 119, Capel St., Dublin.

Ireland (Government of Ireland), 1990. An Environmental Action Plan. Stationery Office, Dublin.

IUCN, 1994. *Parks for Life: Action for Protected Areas in Europe.* IUCN, Geneva.

Meldon, J. and Skehan, C. 1996. *Tourism and the Landscape: Landscape Management by Consensus.* EU LIFE project report. An Taisce and Bord Fáilte.

Mellon, C., and Davidson, L. 1996. Safe and Sound? A health check of Northern Ireland Areas of Special Scientific Interest. Royal Society for the Protection of Birds, Sandy, Bedfordshire.

Mitchell and Associates, 1994. Park Centre Building for Boyne Valley Archaeological Park: Environmental Impact Statement. Submission to Meath County Council, January, 1994 (Planning Ref: 94/47).

Moriarty, C. 1994. Fish Kills in Ireland in 1993. Fishery Leaflet 159, Dept. of the Marine. Dublin.

Nairn, R.G.W. 1992. Areas of Scientific Interest: Time for a rethink. *Ecos 13,* (2).

OPW, 1990. *Killarney National Park. Management Plan.* Office of Public Works, Dublin.

Stapleton, L. 1996. *The State of the Environment in Ireland.* Environmental Protection Agency, Ardcavan, Wexford.

RSPB, 1991. *A Future for Environmentally Sensitive Farming: RSPBSubmission to the Review of Environmentally Sensitive Areas in 1991.* RSPB, Sandy, Beds.

UNESCO (United Nations Educational, Scientific and Cultural Organisation), 1972. Convention concerning the protection of the world cultural and natural heritage. Adopted by the General Conference at its seventeenth session in Paris, 1972. UNESCO, Paris.

UPTCS (Union of Professional and Technical Civil Servants), 1987. *Our Natural Heritage — A Policy for Nature Conservation in Ireland.* Dublin.

Way, L.S., Phil Grice, A. MacKay, C.A. Galbraith, David A. Stroud and M.W. Pienkowski, 1993. *Ireland's Internationally Important Bird Sites: a review of sites for the EC SPA network.* A report commissioned jointly by the National Parks and Wildlife Service, Office of Public Works, Dublin and the Department of the Environment (Northern Ireland), Belfast.

104